This page is intentionaly left blank.

**Cover and Text Design by:** Kim Carroccio

Ghislaine Carriere Raymond & Laurette Leblond

# A LIVING NIGHTMARE

*from the memoirs and stories told*
*by Anneliese Pitt*

# A Living Nightmare

*from the memoirs and stories told*
*by Anneliese Pitt*

GHISLAINE CARRIERE RAYMOND

&

LAURETTE LEBLOND

*To walk through the ruined cities of Germany is to feel an actual doubt about the continuity of civilization.*

\- George Orwell

*Wars are poor chisels for carving out peaceful tomorrows.*

\- Martin Luther King Jr.

# Preface

Many years passed before writing this story. Many have asked why I didn't tell the story before. I had two main reasons for waiting. First, I had to learn to speak and write the English language and second, I hoped to finish my tale with a happy ending. Unfortunately, it was not to be for many years. I resolved to write my story finally. My prime reason to write it was for my sons. So they could understand what I went through, where we came from, and how we came to be in Canada.

Many years have gone by since the Germans trusted communism or fascism. A great deal has changed since then. East Germany has much more to eat since I was there. The trouble that started in the 1930s took a long time to resolve itself. No one in Germany expected to live in luxury after the war. We realized we had done significant damage to other countries. However, many were unaware of what was happening and too young to be accountable for the harm that befell. We wished to be treated like human beings. We knew we had been the enemy, but we hoped that we could trust each other again. Of course, both sides misrepresented the truth.

This is my story, written as I saw East and West Germany and the way I lived for tomorrow. These are my feelings and hopes as a young teenager trying to survive, abandoned, directionless, and surrounded by many who tried as I did only to die of starvation and sickness in post-war Germany.

- Anneliese

# CHAPTER ONE

# Early Childhood

*I* was born Anneliese Möwis. My father, Franz Möwis, was a travelling pedlar in jewelry and precious stones. He was often away for long periods. While still very young, perhaps one year old, my father opened his first barbershop with his brother Henri, in the heart of the city.

In the same building, behind the store, were apartments. Our family lived in one of the six-room apartments. Up to the time I was old enough for school, I slept in my parents' bedroom, which was on the north side of the apartment across from the kitchen. Next to the kitchen, were my sisters' bedrooms. Dora, the eldest, and Elizabeth, the second eldest, shared one room. My third sister, Charlotte (Lotte), occupied the other and later became my roommate.

When I was four or five, I remember going to the park with my sister Lotte. She often ran off to play with boys and left me to explore the park while she was supposed to watch me. At the park, there was a wicket. The woman who worked there often gave balloons to kids. As I stood in front of it, she could not see me. The window was a bit higher than me. I wanted a balloon badly. Since I was out of sight, I jumped up and down, yelling out, "Balloons, balloons, balloons." I continued until she finally opened her window and asked me what I wished. Leaving for a few minutes, she came back with a handful of balloons that I had to blow up myself.

In the meantime, Lotte had searched for me. I must have been there for quite a while playing with my balloons. She became frightened after a lengthy search and went home to tell our parents she could not find me. My parents sent her to inform the police station of my disappearance. By the time I had returned home, the whole neighbourhood was ready to go out and look for me. Everyone had questions about where I had been.

My mother, Berta Möwis, had a job delivering newspapers. She would take me with her to deliver papers. My mother would give me newspapers to place in a door, mailbox or mail slot while she would hurry down the other side of the street. She was often impatient with me. If I made her wait or made a mistake, she would slap me backhanded in the face. It was difficult to satisfy her.

Dora married Paul in 1935 and had a son named Horst in 1936. Not a good man, Paul enjoyed abusing children. My sister Lotte and I had both been assaulted in their kitchen one evening when Dora was looking out for us and had gone to bed early. First, he had his way with Lotte on the kitchen table, and then he turned to me.

*Ann and her mother Berta in Landsberg.*

*Elizabeth and son William in Landsberg.*

Paul had been a professional soldier. He had received a transfer to the General Von Strantz Kaserne in Landsberg. The Kaserne was a big military barrack that sat at the top of a hill. In the summer, it had a breathtaking flower garden in front of the building and three hundred steps encircling the garden in an upside-down "U" shape. I remember playing on those stairs on a walk with my father. An additional barrack by the name of Walter Von Flecks Kaserne, on the outskirts of the city, had less to exhibit. Both of these served professional soldiers.

Paul and Dora expected to live there for the rest of their lives. He died in my early years, but I was too young to know the cause. It had not been a happy marriage for Dora, and she hoped for a new relationship.

Mom and dad accepted their sons-in-law in character and profession as soldiers. My father once said, "It is an excellent occupation if you don't have to fight." This was during peacetime when no one in our family thought of war.

In 1937, at the age of six, I started school. That same year, my sister Elizabeth married Herman Engel, a blacksmith. They moved to Kuestrin, a small town that, to this day, is under Polish leadership about forty-six kilometres from Landsberg. Not long after their move, they had a son named William.

My parents received a telegram one winter morning, a week before Christmas. Mom, who usually was in a foul mood, forgot her anger and sorrows as the telegram announced that Elizabeth and Hermann would arrive with their baby son. Cheerfully, my mother asked, "What is today? Just look at me, I am still in the middle of baking the Christmas cakes and cookies. Isn't it like always, when special visitors like our daughter come to visit, we are always busy," she continued but talking more to herself. Baking was not important to my mother, but holding that baby boy in her arms was.

We had not seen Elizabeth and Hermann since their wedding day. It was a pleasant occasion for us all, especially for my parents to see their grandson. Mom sent Lotte to Dora's, across the Warthe, to invite them for supper.

While sitting around the table after supper, Elizabeth mentioned that they had not been able to have their honeymoon. She asked mom if she would mind keeping the baby while they went away. "I know it sounds rather funny," a timid Elizabeth continued, "but Hermann has to report to the recruiting center in Frankfurt-Oder and join the army. That is only two weeks from now. I would like to stay with him over the Christmas holiday so that he does not get too lonely." Elizabeth's voice sounded both excited and apologetic. As she spoke, she kept looking from her husband to mom.

Smiling and understanding, mom replied, "You did not need to elaborate so Elizabeth. Of course, you can leave the baby with us. We would love to have little Willie, regardless of what the reason might be."

It was exciting to have everyone sitting around the table, enjoying a family reunion. Everyone, including the boys, laughed and enjoyed themselves.

Elizabeth and Hermann planned to take the last train out of Landsberg headed to Hamburg to start their honeymoon off in a grand style. As Dad was getting ready to take Elizabeth and Hermann to the station, he reassured them not to worry about their son. He was sure the baby was in good hands. I thought with mom looking so happy and smiling, of course, it would be no trouble. She adored her grandchildren and especially that they were boys.

My mother once told me that during her pregnancy, she yearned for a son and was very disappointed when they told her I was a girl. All her labour pains and difficulties she had to suffer during the last three weeks of pregnancy would have been rewarding had I been a boy. Growing up, I noticed she did not play with me the way she did with my sisters' babies, nor did I feel the love and affection she showed them. Mom played with little Willie until he squeaked with joy like a piglet and all the time, I pretended the play included me too.

I stood by, my mouth opened in awe, watching mom bathe the baby, kiss his little hands, and pat his tiny rosy bottom. How I longed for the same love from her. Only God knew how much it hurt me to see that she cared more for the babies than she did for me. My mother was a good woman. However, I did not understand her lack of affection for me. She meant no harm when she said to me one day, "I wished for a baby boy so much, but God did not answer my prayers." I don't know how she intended for me to absorb this, but it hurt me very much.

I felt my little heart overflowing with love toward my mother. I wondered if she had ever done the same things to me or loved me in the same way, as I was too young to remember any of it. My mother did not like to be kissed nor any of my affection towards her. She didn't fuss over me. Had she shared an affectionate word once in a while, my heart would have jumped with joy. She tried to show her affection in other ways.

On one such occasion, she bought me a doll. My only toy, ever. The doll, made of paper-maché, was soiled at one point. Wanting it clean, I bathed it in the water. The paper deteriorated. That was the end of my toys. She thought it would have made me happy when all I wanted was to feel her arms around me.

My mother found me to be a challenge and was impatient with me. At times, she would check my school lessons and strike me in the face when I made mistakes. It would make my nose bleed. I would remember her violence but not the lessons she was trying to help me memorize.

I would spend time in my room where I would sit by the window to daydream. I would wonder why my mother was so cold towards me. I questioned if she had treated my sisters in the same fashion when they were young and also if they found it hard growing up. Sometimes I believed they did. They never reminisced about their earlier days. Now they were all married, except for Lotte and I. Dora and Elizabeth lived the life they had chosen away from my mother's eyes. Perhaps, I was to blame for my misfortune. No matter how much I reflected on this, I was unable to find any answers.

As for my father, who was rarely at home, he was too busy to show his affection for me. He would never find time to sit me on his lap and put his arms around me. I felt so unhappy and lonely at home. I was anemic, small, neglected.

I enjoyed staying overnight at a friend's house or one of my parents' friends' houses. I was never eager to come back home. It felt empty. I usually had to fend for myself. It was so much nicer at Aunt Clara's, my dad's oldest sister, where I sometimes spent my summer school holidays. I looked forward to being away from home and Lotte. I don't recall having trouble getting along with Dora or Elizabeth. However, Lotte and I could not stand the sight of each other. In a way, I couldn't blame her as she was older than I and looked more mature.

Very often, I would come home for lunch to find an empty apartment. There was nothing for me to eat. I would run down to one of the shops and beg for some food. The neighbourhood bakery usually gave me a bag of cake trimmings, the dried pieces they had removed from their cakes before selling them. The ice cream parlour would give me their dried cones without the ice cream.

At eight years old, I was still a young child in comparison with Lotte, who was now sixteen. Lotte was dating after school. My mother was not pleased when I told her. She did not approve of dating at such a young age. Unfortunately, my mother had strict rules and became more abusive when my father was away.

After my telling on my sister, my mother used the six-streamer on her. A painful punishment, the six-streamer looks like a baton at one end and has six leather bands hanging from the other end. Lotte had trouble accepting the flogging. She swore to pay me back one day. She sure did when I least expected it.

Long after I had forgotten the incident, my parents had gone out and left me alone at home with Lotte. She pulled out the six-streamer and whipped me good. "You will get a lot more if you dare to tell mom or dad about this beating, you, you ugly duckling," she screamed at me in anger. Lotte and I never forgot the pain these floggings inflicted on us.

The term "ugly duckling" quickly spread in the neighbourhood. Even at school, the name-calling continued, particularly with the boys on the street. The more I got upset about it, the more they teased me. Had I been strong and wise, I could have shown them who was ugly.

Following that name-calling, I often studied my image in the mirror. I would examine my long pale face topped with a bushel of blond hair that refused to cover my forehead due to an ill-placed cowlick, long nose, thin lips and stare into my crossed blue eyes. I have a lazy eye that falls to the side and impairs my vision. I had had surgery on my eye as a young child before starting school, but the results were poor. Despite all of this, I could not see anything disagreeable with my looks. Could I help if my sister and now the rest of the kids didn't like my appearance? Nature made me that way.

Our parents were quite neglectful. However, Lotte was quite rebellious. She would often get herself in trouble. At one point, she ended up incarcerated for stealing. The city jail was on the opposite side of our street. Often, as I got ready for bed, I would see her through the window waving at me.

The last memories I have at home with Lotte was when she became pregnant. After this, she moved away to Dora's apartment. She made room in her kitchen for a bed where Lotte would stay until the baby was born. In that same room, she eventually delivered a baby girl named Anita. My sister did not raise Anita. After the delivery, Lotte moved to Berlin, where she studied and worked at the Robert Koch Hospital. At the time, I did not understand what was happening.

I was so pleased with the summer holidays approaching. Each year before the holidays, a doctor would visit the school and select students to send to different parts of Germany for the summer. They selected me under the category of underprivileged, the poor and anemic looking children. Having been to Pomerania and Schlesien in previous years, this was my third time chosen. I enjoyed imagining what was going to happen.

That day, I took a letter home requesting my parents' permission to let me go for five weeks to Danzig-Ohra on the Baltic Sea. They agreed to let me go. Mom thought it would do me some good to be away and amongst strangers. The letter given to my parents had to return to the doctor. I was thrilled at the thought of my departure from Landsberg.

When the time came for me to leave my hometown, my mother accompanied me to the station. We said our goodbyes while the conductor signalled the engineer. The train started to roll; slowly at first and then gradually gaining speed. I waved to my mother until I could no longer see her. I was very excited about my adventure and looked forward to the things that would take place. I also looked forward to meeting the people who would be my foster parents for the next five weeks. I was too excited to shed a tear as some of the other children did.

Danzig, a major Baltic seaport situated on a branch of the Vistula river, has quite the history. It belonged first to Russia, then Poland, then Germany and back to Poland. A lovely city with exquisite medieval architecture, I would spend my summer holiday in one of its suburbs, Ohra.

In 1939, Hitler demanded the city of Danzig return to German control. Poland rejected. My summer holiday would end, and I had to return home. Germany had declared war.

My foster parents were wonderful people. I began to get comfortable and started to enjoy my new surroundings. The food was different from what I was accustomed to. I enjoyed it very much. I shed a lot of tears when my foster mother informed me that I would be returning home sooner than planned. It was two days before my departure. At first, I thought she was teasing me and later considered that perhaps, I was too much trouble. I soon realized it was the reality. I tried to convince her to keep me until the weekend. I later understood that it was not her choice to make. It was our Fuehrer. I often thought of them and still do to this day.

War is a hard and cruel thing to live through. I did not understand much about our politics. Little was taught to us to grasp the history of Danzig and Germany. I wanted to belong, but we were not Polish. We did not speak the language. We were Germans under Polish supervision. I knew that I had to go back home because of the war. I was sent by train out of the city along with the other children from Landsburg. Sadly, the residents of Danzig were not permitted to leave.

Back in Landsberg, my mother was waiting for me at the station. She had heard the bad news but refused to talk about it. I found her to be irritable and lacking interest when I would speak of my holiday. How I wished I could have shared it with her, but she acted as if she rather not have me around. We hurried home along Station Street, around the corner onto Ritch Strauss (Main Street). The area was not one I often visited, and it was far from our playgrounds. However, I found many things to be bizarre both on the streets and in the store windows.

My mother did not mention to me that during my absence, Uncle Henri had visited us. I heard of it in a greeting from my dad. "We have a surprise for you," dad said as he pointed with his finger towards the living room. He followed me in as I looked around the room. I couldn't see anything of a surprise. Dad helped me look and signalled me to look upon the drape's rail. There, astonished, I saw the most beautiful large blue, red and yellow coloured parrot.

"Uncle Henri left the bird for you. He picked it up on one of his trips to the morning land."

"I can't believe this dad, that this is my very own bird to care for."

"What a cute bird," I thought to myself, "to have as a playmate." The bird was mainly kept in the barbershop. On days the business was closed, my father would bring it back to the apartment. Unfortunately, the bird did not live long. It was disposed of with the morning trash and never mentioned again.

Shortly after this episode, we were awakened in the night by a heavy smell of smoke. My uncle Henri arrived to let us know there was a bad fire in the Jewish neighbourhood. He was on his way to see. He believed it was the Jewish Synagogue. Promising he would return in the morning to give us more news, he left to investigate. In the morning, we received news that the temple had burned to the ground, along with several nearby dwellings. Uncle Henri, who had not returned, had been picked up by the police.

Religion was never discussed or practiced in our home. My mother was Christian; my father and uncle were Jewish. My father was close to our family doctor, Doctor Friedlander, who was also Jewish. He would join us for dinner periodically and played Chess with my dad.

The friction that existed between my parents was with the Nazi party. My father wanted nothing to do with it, while my mother would sneak away to our neighbours or to Dora's to listen to the speeches. She loved listening to the radio when the Fuehrer or Doctor Herman Goering spoke. My mother, as well as many Germans, was blinded by his promises. The children were to stay very quiet at this time and not interrupt the adults.

# CHAPTER TWO

# Father Captured by Nazis

*I* was so busy talking to my girlfriend Rosa, sitting next to me, that I did not hear Miss Meier call my name. "Möwis, Anneliese, she repeated, would you like to stay after school?" Ashamed, I stood up and nodded no. I did not want to stay after school. My mind was on my summer plans. It was the last day of the school year.

"Your father should send you to high school. You pass too easily," she said when I walked to her desk to receive my report card.

"Thank you. I will tell my father," I replied.

I remained serious, but it wouldn't have taken much to make me giggle. I took a brief look at my report card. I could only hope my dad would be as pleased with the grades.

My father had promised to purchase a bicycle if my grades were satisfactory. Perhaps, I should share with him what Miss Meier suggested, I thought. Even after I had been warned not to, I continued to chat with Rosa. I had to share my joy with her.

"With a report card like that, as sure as my name is Rosa, the bike is as good as yours," said Rosa, giving me more encouragement.

"If I didn't have to leave town today, Anneliese Möwis, I would certainly keep you after school," shouted Miss Meier as the school bell rang.

Just like a flock of sheep, each student tried to be first out of the classroom. Miss Meier attempted to regain control of the class and show us how to leave the classroom appropriately. Rosa invited me to go swimming in the afternoon. Winking, I told her I would be too busy. My father and I were going shopping for a bike. I laughed. We then bid each other goodbye.

We always parted at the Mauer Gasse (Masonry Lane). Rosa went through the Backry Gasse (Bakery Lane), while I continued along the Mauer-Gasse until I reached the Richt Strasse (Main Street). Our address was 71 Richt Strasse. At my left stood the back of the big city jail with its iron-barred windows. On the other side of the lane were small houses, a bakery, an ice cream parlour, a fish store, and the barbershop. My father rarely worked there. My Uncle Henri usually supervised the barbershop. Most of the time, my father was gone peddling precious stones.

To my delight, my father was home. He was to look after me while my mother was in the hospital for surgery. Turning the corner on Richt Strasse, I saw people gathered in front of the stores. From where I stood, I couldn't tell with certainty which store. As I got closer, I became more anxious. I could see they were in front of my uncle and father's barbershop. I rushed and pushed through the crowd until I reached the front of the building, leading to the door. Only then did I see the two secret police step outside, followed by my father. I recall screaming, "Da," but no sound came out. I stood still, frozen in time.

My father stood in front of me, his hands bound together. The sparkle was missing from his eyes. His mouth displayed a twisted smile. Never in my entire life will I forget that look. It broke my heart. If he spoke to me, I didn't hear it. I don't believe he did. The two secret police behind him pushed him on, toward the car waiting on the side of the street. He completely ignored me, did not look at me. It was as if I was not there. I always wondered if it had been on purpose. Later, I realized, he probably saved my life at this time.

Seeing them push dad like that made me understand this was serious and that they were taking him away from us. With all my strength, I tried to reach my father and grab his bound hands through the crowd, but I couldn't reach him. With one hand, the secret police pushed my father into the car and with the other one, with all his strength, he swung a blow to my face. I lost my balance and fell backward onto the ground. Blood rushed out of my nose and mouth. Through tears, I watched the car roll away down the street. "Da, oh da, please come back. Please don't leave me alone," I sobbed with my head on the warm cement sidewalk.

He couldn't hear me anymore. I tried to make sense of what had happened. Dabbing my bloody nose and eyes with my skirt, I told myself, he had to leave us. Then I heard Mrs. Flegel's unwanted voice, "He helped the Jews. He cut their hair. I saw it with my very own eyes. He gave them food and even let them into his apartment in the early morning hours. I saw it just after my husband set out for work. I couldn't believe it. I told him what I saw going on from the window. Jews were entering his shop as if they lived there."

I should have known that nothing passed unnoticed by her. She had a poisoned tongue like a snake and eyes like a hawk. I gave her a daggered look when I got up from the sidewalk, unassisted, and staggered into the apartment.

In the entrance stood Frau Schultz, my best friend's mother. Her arms reached out for me, but she didn't dare touch me. I passed her in the doorway without talking or even taking notice. She followed me into the apartment. I proceeded to the bathroom and tried to clean myself. In the mirror, I looked more like a blood-smeared butcher than a sad, young girl. I washed my hot, sore face with cool water and then went back to the front room.

Mrs. Schultz patiently waited for me. Now I hated and mistrusted everyone, including Frau Schultz. I asked her what had happened, expecting all the details of my father's abduction. "I don't really know, dear," she whispered timidly as though she could read the look in my eyes. "I don't believe what the people are saying, especially Mrs. Flegel," she continued cautiously.

"What did she say?" I asked Mrs. Schultz angrily, hearing Mrs. Flegel's name mentioned.

"She spoke of sabotage and said she knows that your father was a traitor to the Reich." She replied in such a low voice that I could hardly understand what she was saying. She looked down at the floor, shamefully, and added, "All have some kind of story to tell, but no one seems to know."

I stood there with only one thought in mind; revenge on this terrible Mrs. Flegel. How I now despised this woman. Mrs. Schultz asked if I wanted something to eat for lunch, but I nodded no. She got up from her chair and prepared some food for me, anyway. I couldn't eat. I only nibbled at the bread while Mrs. Schultz washed the morning dishes. Before leaving, she asked if I wanted to go to her place. I thanked her. Absentmindedly, I told her I was fine and could not stand to leave home just now. After she left the apartment, I lay on the chesterfield and cried myself to sleep.

The bad news spread quickly. Even to Dora's place across the river. When Dora came to see me, I was awake and sitting by the window. It was my favourite place to sit to sort out my thoughts. Dora never asked me anything, she likely knew more than I did. She only asked me when it happened. "When I got home from school," I answered slowly. She too invited me to go with her, but again I refused. I much preferred to stay home. Perhaps, if dad returned, he would not find the apartment empty.

Sleep would not come to me that night. I was deeply confused about all the activities of the past few days. My eyes burned from crying and staring in the dark. I could not find the reasoning behind these events and worried often. I would wonder how dad would defend himself if it came to his life or someone else's and if he had joined the forces. I think he knew his chances of remaining alive would have been slim to none in the war. I believed him when he said he preferred waiting it out at home.

A cold shiver ran down my spine when I thought of what would happen to him. As I closed my eyes, Uncle Henri came to mind. He had been taken away by the secret police two weeks prior. I imagined my uncle Henri with the many little scars imprinted on his face from an explosion of a hand grenade, scars from the First World War. Now, he had to relive war again.

Uncle Henri was not a handsome man, but he had a heart of gold. He had helped mothers with children escape when the fire was set to the Jewish temple. He would have known that most of the women and children were Jewish. They were human, like him. His first thoughts were to help and not to divide because of their religion. At the time, he could not have known the fire was set by the Nazis. Now, he was gone. I know he meant no harm to the party. He only did what, I think, anyone else with a good heart would have done.

Slowly, I realized that not all of our Fuehrers' doings had been good. There was nothing left for us to do except to wait and see what time would bring us. It was too late for us to leave the country. If they could have, my parents would never have left their country of Austria, where they had the same rights as their fellow citizens, or so they thought. Now both Henri and my father had been captured, and I wondered if I would ever see them again.

When I awoke the following morning, I had an awful taste in my mouth. My body felt heavy, and my eyes were swollen. Then, it all came back to me. It was not a bad dream, and reality set in. Not entirely convinced, I went to my parent's bedroom to find the door still open, with no one inside. The pillows and the white cover on top of the bed were untouched. Dad had not returned during the night, as I had hoped. My feelings were bitter and hurt. I was so confused.

I could no longer bear the silence in the apartment. I paced the floor. As I walked to the front, I looked out of the window. I heard my friend Lore say, "Good morning," in her strong accent. It was hard for me to accept the truth. There was only emptiness in my heart. The dreams of yesterday, which remained, seemed much less important now. I felt I had no one to turn to and could not face anyone.

Until my mother returned from the hospital, where she was healing from surgery, I remained at home until four-thirty in the afternoon. Then, I went to my sister Dora's for supper, who, since her wedding, had lived across the river. Sometimes, I would spend the night there, but most often would return home. When I did spend the night, I would get up at seven and leave her house when she left for work. Her son Horst went to kindergarten.

Two weeks passed before mom came back home from the hospital. I had not seen her since she had first gone there. My sister Dora had made me promise not to visit alone. She did not trust me to keep quiet. She thought I might tell about Father and make her feel worse. I was never told why she was hospitalized. When I saw her next, I felt sorry for her. She was a tall, big-boned woman who had fair hair and large features. Her demeanour was overpowering, strict and often abusive. When she returned home from the hospital, she was weak, pale and thin.

Nothing seemed the same anymore. Everything was dull, empty and uneasy. Mom sat at the window, staring ahead at nothing. I spent my time doing housework, roaming the neighbourhood, or sitting in front of the barbershop. Somehow, I did not feel the coldness of the kids around the street.

I saw Rosa just before school restarted. I had not seen her during my holidays. We met in a store. "Rosa!" I called out.

"Hey," she barely replied.

"Is something the matter?" I asked.

She apologized, "I am sorry, Annie. It's not my fault I have ignored you. My mother thinks you're a bad influence. Since your father left ..."

Mrs. Schultz must have felt threatened at the possibility of being ostracised for associating with my family. Rosa attempted to explain, searching for the right words. I cut her off in an angry outburst and left, crying all the way home. I felt helpless. After this, I locked myself in my room a great deal. I needed Rosa as my friend. Who could I turn to for support? I looked forward to school, hoping things would be easier to take.

# CHAPTER THREE

# The War Years

On the first day of school, waiting for the bell to ring in the schoolyard, I noticed a group of girls putting their heads together and pointing at me. One of them called me a communist and a traitor to the Reich. My blood boiling, I grabbed her hair with both hands and pulled her down. The other kids gathered around us to watch the fight, ignoring the school bell. From the school building, Miss Meier came to lead the children in. "Anneliese Möwis," she shouted. I was so furious and blinded by anger that she had to use force to get me off the girl. Miss Meier asked who had started the fight. I tried to explain. She sent me home to change and clean myself up.

At home, my mother was waiting for me, "You can't go around hitting others because they hurt your feelings. I hear gossip in the store. I hear our neighbours talking about us, but I don't hit them. I deal with things on my own. You have to learn to smile at them and walk away. This is the only way we can strike back and protect ourselves."

I knew then that I would never be able to do what she asked of me. How could I smile when they were so wrong? Could I not defend myself? I realize now that I was not the only one hurt. My mother was also suffering and probably Dora too.

The war was on, and there were many newcomers to Landsberg from Berlin. There had been many bombings, and many families were moving in with relatives. The children came to our school. They told us of the nights of terror in the air raid shelters and destruction. We could not know of the fear they had experienced as there had been no bombings in our city.

Christmas that year was very sad. There was no comfort for my mother. Often, both she and Dora would break into tears. My sister Lotte, who was now in Berlin to study, did not come for Christmas but did come for the New Year. Christmas gifts did not exist for me. Mom's thoughts were with Dad. We all wondered what he was going through. If he could have been with us for Christmas, it would have been the best present to receive. Dora was also thinking of her husband.

I looked forward to seeing my sister Lotte that year. She was not pleased that we had not told her about our father. After the first week, she became irritated and angrily burst out at Mother, "Do you have to cry every time someone mentions Dad?" My mother looked surprised but did not answer.

During her visit, Lotte told me over and over again how much she loved her work at the hospital in Berlin, and that perhaps one day, she could study to become a doctor. As her visit neared the end, she said, "I am delighted to go back to work. It is tough to stay here without Dad. We would have had a lot to talk about, discussing my work."

After Lotte's Christmas leave was over, Mother asked her to stay at home. She refused. My sister was well established at the hospital and due to return to Berlin. She would not be happy at home with my mother watching over her. In Berlin, she was free to do as she pleased after her duties.

Mother waited day after day for news of my father, but none ever came. After the Easter holiday, she decided to move closer to Dora. She found a small apartment on Wessel Street and began selling some of the furniture from our home and store. We needed the money now that my father was gone and my mother was not working. Despite the money invested in the barbershop, only a pittance was raised from its sale.

After the move, she began to feel better and mentioned Dad's name, less and less. She asked me not to speak of him. "If he had done what he was told to do, he would not have been picked up," she would say. My mother looked for work as a cook, which she had been in the past.

As for me, I enjoyed swimming in the nearby river and playing in the park, near the bridge, that led to our new home. That fall, I changed school and made new friends. I often thought of Rosa. She was still the best friend I ever had.

My mother eventually found a job at I.G. Farben. This was a large conglomerate that developed chemicals and pharmaceutical products. They used Russian prisoners to build the plant in Landsberg. Afterwards, the conglomerate used the prisoners for experimentation. I never stopped to think about what the facility was for. Everything that happened there was kept strictly confidential. No one dared to take any information out of the plant.

When Mom worked, I did everything except what I should have done. She did not mind working as a cook's helper. She had little responsibilities, and it kept her occupied. Although I did visit a few times, I did not find anything interesting there. Occasionally, I would help peel potatoes. The cook would warn me not to walk around with a knife in my hand; it could have been deadly.

While I was there, I saw prisoners being served their evening meal. A German soldier watched over two war prisoners while they picked up a big boiling kettle of potatoes and carried it out. One of the prisoners stuck his hand in the boiling water and grabbed a potato. They would have beaten and shot him had he been exposed. All I saw were dirty, skinny men being pushed around and bullied. At the time, I did not realize the pain they were suffering.

When mom took me shopping one particular weekend, I noticed a sign over the counter in the Becker-Becker bakery. It read, "Attention All Jews. The sale of white bread and cake of any kind is strictly prohibited and severely punishable." When I asked mom about the sign, she said she hadn't noticed the sign before. She did not know how long it had been there. I asked to join her for future shopping trips. By the following weekend, another sign, written in the same black letters, accompanied the first one. "Attention All Jews. Jews are not allowed to be served in this store at any time." It was signed by the Reich, in the same way as the first one.

During the following weeks, I noticed similar signs in every store that supplied the needs of the people. I started wondering where Jewish people could obtain these items since every citizen lived from the ration card. Still, I saw Jewish people obtaining their ration card when my mother sent me to get ours. I should have known that this was only a trick of the Nazis to get a hold of the Jews.

I recall seeing Jewish people leaving dad's barbershop with a parcel of food in return for their ration card. I often wonder what was really going on in that store. There were so many things I didn't understand. The cruel-hearted with nothing better to do than to gossip all day, like Mrs. Flegal, could bring the Reich's unwanted attention to someone's doorstep. They would spread stories heard from one neighbour and from there, to another. Someone could then report to a Brownshirt like her husband. Brownshirts were part of a military organization that could resort to brute force and methods for terrorizing. These occurrences were eerily similar to what happened with my father.

# CHAPTER FOUR

# Russians

*I* loved my native city of Landsberg on de Wartha. It was situated 95 miles east of where they built the big stone wall in Berlin. Landsberg was the name of the city, and Wartha the name of the river that flows through it. In 1939, Landsberg was a prominent trade and transportation center. The river played an important part in the economy for its 48,053 residents. Now, it is owned by Poland and known as the city of Gorzow. If only in my heart, the city was important enough to obtain a place in history.

During the war, many citizens fled the city, abandoned their homes and businesses. Daily, individuals took their most precious belongings in small bags and carried them on their shoulders, hoping to find safety elsewhere. Others pushed small wooden carts, loaded with household paraphernalia, with the hope of finding a better life. As a young girl, I noticed many families were running from something. I did not understand this common daily sight. I never stopped to think about where they came from or where they were going.

By the time Russia liberated the East Germans from the Nazis, women and children waited in fear in our city. It was January when the Russians first appeared, not long after my fourteenth birthday, which was on January 9th. In March of 1945, I saw Polish soldiers for the first time. They rode on horseback carrying their flags and singing and had come to take Landsberg. We no longer had radios or newspapers. Still, the news spread in only a few days.

It was difficult to believe that Landsberg on de Wartha no longer existed in the Atlas. I was born there and lived there until fourteen years of age. When I returned to my hometown in 1968, I found it to be a dangerous journey. I feared the Russians and Polish. Although I was not wanted on criminal charges, as far as I knew, I worried they might find something wrong with my papers. Since then, I've thought twice before going back to visit my hometown.

One day, my mother and older sister Dora decided to leave our home and to follow thousands of refugees already on the highways, railway stations and streets. We never made it to the railway station. People of all ages blocked the entrance to the railway. The Germans were still on the warpath. They exploded the bridge that crossed the river, trying to stop the Russian tanks from crossing over. We returned home and waited for the deliberation by the Russians from the German Nazi Power.

If we had left the city that day, our life would have have been different. We had little left when the Russians came. Part of the town was burnt down. They took the remainder of our resources. We no longer had power for light or to listen to the radio, freshwater, gas, food and doctors. They raped women, killed the elderly and anyone else who resisted their brutality.

To get food, we became raiders, and we stole. First, we went to the farmers' fields where we dug up different kinds of root cellars and mounds of vegetable preserves that had been covered over for the winter. A few weeks later, I met a girlfriend, and we decided to go forage in the city for food. We raided empty apartments people had abandoned. She would go on one floor while I would take another.

In one of the apartments, I was confronted for the first time by a Russian soldier. He pushed me in a corner and made me face the wall with a gun at my temple. Then, he raped me. I suffered through it with cries of pain. I was extremely terrified. At fourteen, I only had a faint understanding of the birds and the bees. As I fulfilled his demands, he kept repeating, "Good girl. Good girl". Once he was done having his way, he helped me find food. Although the war had ended, it seemed like this was the beginning of mine.

In April of that year, my mother could no longer afford our apartment. We moved in with my sister Dora. At this time, Russian soldiers, accompanied by women known as "Flinten Weiber (gun girls)," would go from door to door to seize people's personal belongings. These Russians took everything we owned. They emptied our cupboards and closets. They only allowed us one change of clothes and nothing else. The piano was too big to take out of the door, so they decided to throw it out through the window. We kept personal documents in the piano and lost all proof of our identity with its destruction. It was hard to see the piano destroyed.

One day, the Russians called the whole neighbourhood to meet in the garden. The garden, situated off the back lane of Dora's apartment building, would be the setting for a public execution. The Russian soldiers asked who was the owner of a flag they had found in one of the apartments. It was a Swastika, the Nazi emblem. After a long pause, one man slowly raised his hand. Having admitted his wrongdoing, the Russians used him as a lesson to us all. They threw him on the ground and yelled at him in Russian. We could not understand a word they were saying. Then, horses were placed on each side of the man and tied to his legs. People were hiding their faces. My mother covered my eyes, but I could still hear the piercing screams. It took just a few seconds. It was gory and cruel. We all left as fast as we could without speaking. Everyone was heavy with fear.

That year, Russia agreed to give Poland a large piece of East Germany, including my home town. Soon after, they assigned the remaining population to work. Women were taken on farms, streets, or hospitals to work for the Russians. My tasks entailed cleaning and burying the dead. I also helped with cleaning the hospital for wounded soldiers. My mother changed my age to sixteen so that I could work instead of giving blood, which was what the younger teenagers were required to do. I did not return home for days. I slept on the cement floor in a basement and ate at the hospital. My mother and sister chose one of these days when I was away to escape town with Horst, leaving me behind. At that time, anyone who did not want to become a Polish citizen had to leave Landsberg on da Wartha.

On my return from work, no one could tell me where I could find my mother. As time went on, the search for my mother became less promising. In the camps, I found shelter for a night or two. There was nobody to protect me. Everyone in my surroundings seemed to be leaving or preparing to do so. Although it seemed impossible to live on, I did not want to die like a rat on a sidewalk.

# CHAPTER FIVE

# Escape to Berlin

*A*lone at night, while everyone was asleep, I fled. I couldn't waste any more time trying to find my mother and sister in Landsberg. I set my hopes on Berlin and finding them at Lotte's in-laws, in Wilhelmminhof Strasse. I pushed away any doubts that I would find them. It took me most of the night and most of the following day, to reach the city. I walked, ran and rode the train. At this particular time, only the Russians were allowed to ride inside the train. I had to sit on the top or hold on to one of the ladders.

Years after this journey, one moment stood out in my memory. As a group of us walked single file, across the frozen shore of the river, I noticed a woman leaning back in a snowbank. No one glanced at her. In my curiosity, I approached her, seeing the baby she was holding to her breast. Neither was moving. They were frozen in time, having died there. Nothing to be done, I resumed a place in the procession to Berlin.

It was my first time seeing Berlin. In my childish imagination, I believed the city would be just like I had dreamt it, but to my surprise, it was not even close. Much of it had been destroyed and burned, mostly, by enemy bombings. I slowly became accustomed to disappointments. My expectations were not what the reality of the situation was.

In Lichtenberg, I asked where to find Oberschöneweide. After receiving the necessary information, it took me one more day to get to the house. I could not believe it when I saw it. The whole neighbourhood was in shambles and ruins, shattering any hope left.

I asked the people passing by if I was on the correct street. I was at the right address. (Lichtenberg and Oberschöneweide are boroughs of Berlin, Germany). I asked around to see if someone knew where they had gone or if they were still living. Looking among the ruins, I thought perhaps I would find something that would give me a clue, a bit of information or some hope. Tears of disappointment dropped to the ground among old stovepipes and wires. The bodies of the people I was looking for, were covered in earth and ashes.

I had limited knowledge surrounding the air raids and understood little of people's fears and losses. My experience in Landsberg was nothing compared to the frightful nights in Berlin. I believed the Russians acted the same there as they did in Landsberg. They were the conquerors, and we were all considered Nazis, their enemy.

My mind worked desperately and created question upon question. "What will happen to me now? Where do I go from here?"

An older woman approached me, "Are you looking for something?"

"Yes," I replied. I hesitated to ask. I was expecting, "I am sorry. I can't help you." However, I could not stay on the street all night. I asked her if she knew Mrs. Schweitzer. She said she did and asked if they were related to me. I quickly explained that they were my brother-in-law's parents. After clarifying why I was looking for them, the older lady invited me to her home.

"I have not much to offer you, but if you would like to spend the night with me, you will be safe," she proposed in a friendly manner. The woman walked bent over. She told me she was Mrs. Shweitzer, but folks around here called her Mrs. Wiesel. "I don't blame them as I make my living like one," she said. I was so relieved. I now knew one person in Berlin.

When we reached her place, I understood why she thought I wouldn't like it. Her little home was no more than a hole amongst the ruins. It had no door, no windows, and all the light came through the entrance. Inside her home, I saw an open fireplace with a bench beside it. In one of the four corners of the room, I saw an old rusty bed and some of her belongings. There, she slept during the night.

"I eat where and when I find it, and now, I am sorry to say, I have no food to offer you," she explained.

"It's alright," I comforted her. Even though I was famished, I would not accept any food from the woman who barely survived from one day to the next.

She spoke of her children. Her sons died, serving the German army. Her daughters, once happily married, had disappeared in this cruel world.

"I came back, from Chemnitz, a city 181 miles south of Berlin", she offered. "I believed, like you, that I would find one of my daughters here. I believe that under these stones, lies my daughter and her two children. I also know that I will watch over them until I close my eyes." I asked about my sister, Lotte. She told me she had not heard from her in a long time.

The old lady spoke slowly but surely. I didn't dare touch the bitterness of her wounded heart concerning her daughters or my sister. Otherwise, I would have asked her how she knew her daughter and grandchildren were under the rubble. While Mrs. Shweitzer kept on talking, my mind wandered off to my mother. I felt my eyes heavy and burning from exhaustion and fell asleep.

It was still dark outside, but the pains of hunger would not let me sleep any longer. I remembered the Russian prisoner stealing the hot potatoes out of the kettle when I was a younger child, thinking then how stupid they could be. I wished now I could put a hot potato in my mouth to quiet my painful stomach.

In the early morning, as the sun came up, Mrs. Schweitzer asked if I had any plans, once I left. I had no answer to offer, no future to await with pleasure. I could not think of anywhere for me to go.

"I know a refugee camp in Lichtenberg. Perhaps, you can find a place. There may even be food for you," she suggested.

"It's worth a try," I answered and thanked the old woman for her help. I hoped to return soon, to spend her last days with her and offer her the comfort of friendship and a bit of food.

It was late afternoon the next day before I managed to reach the refugee camp Mrs. Schweitzer had mentioned. I walked through an open gate, across a big square, which to me looked like a schoolyard. Straight ahead, there stood a big dwelling, with smaller ones on each side, overshadowed by a tree. I assumed the larger building would be where the refugees lived.

Then, coming from one of the smaller houses, I heard a mouth-piece guiding the singing Russians. Not knowing what I had to do before entering a refugee camp, I walked straight into the big dwelling. There, I opened the big door. They were having supper. An evil smell hit me while I was standing still in the entrance. In the middle of the vast hall, I found women and children of all ages gathered around two Russian soldiers standing near a kettle placed on a chair. Here, they handed out the rations for the evening.

No one spared a look in my direction, nor cared that I was standing there. I felt too pitiful to move from the door. I could smell the steam from the kettle, but could not make out what it was. I only knew it was something to satisfy my stomach. Hunger got the best of me and chased away my shyness. Slowly, I approached the steaming kettle. I felt like I was dreaming. Walking to the front of all the others standing in line, I heard the growl of the people. It was as if they were dogs, and I had come to take their bones away. Perhaps, I just wanted to smell the food from the kettle. Under normal circumstances, I would have avoided it altogether. The smell was not inviting. The hungry people that filled the room thought otherwise. One of the women pushed me away as I tried to take her place in line. I had no thoughts nor emotions. My eyes became blurry as I felt the pangs of hunger.

I could see a little girl standing beside me. She offered me her bowl. I had nothing to hold the soup that the Russians were serving. "I had my supper. Take it. They will not give you anything without a bowl," she instructed. I hesitated, thinking I was likely going to deprive her of her food. She kept holding the bowl under my nose. I grabbed the bowl, hoping I wouldn't be too late to get it filled with the warm liquid. I finally stood in front of the kettle, where one of the Russians filled it with soup. There was no need for a spoon to eat this soup. I drank it slowly and felt it soothing my stomach. It felt good, even if it was watery with only a few cabbage leaves and a piece of rye bread.

Shortly after having my ration, the two Russians smiled, leaving with the empty kettle. They seemed pleased that we waited for them to come. The anticipation of their return with our next meal gave them a sense that we valued them. They knew too well that they were the conquerors. I had no respect for Russians.

In the hall, stood a long wooden table, where the refugees sat and ate their food. I sat down on the benches to one side of the table and found myself able to look around. In the four corners of the big hall, women and children, young and old, sat on wooden frame beds, some filled with straw. Their belongings, which they used to cover themselves, were few. Children sat on the floor, or they lay in their beds too weak to play or stand on their little feet. Their bodies were so thin. Their eyes were sunken, big from hunger, fear, and fright for the next day.

The lives of refugees were sad and harsh. The only ones who could understand the hardships and fear were the refugees themselves. At fourteen years old, the only way for me to describe it was desperation. Perhaps, adults had a different perspective. Everyone tried to live for "tomorrow" and hoped that it would be better than the past. How many more tomorrows would we wait for and survive? No one knew, but we all looked forward to it.

When the time came to find myself a bed, I selected one at the far end of the hall. It was an iron bed that only had springs, no mattress. A woman and her child, who owned a feather cover and pillow, slept in the next bed. In view, high up on the four walls where no one could reach them, were little windows. For the sake of flies, the main door remained closed. The air inside the camp was damp and stagnant with an awful, overwhelming smell of unwashed bodies.

It felt good to lay down on a bed and stretch out, though not for long. The springs dug into my body. I was exhausted, but sleep would not come. My thoughts circled on my father, mother and sisters. Without them, I wondered what would become of me. Eventually, I found sleep.

Later in the night, I awoke frozen. I tried to pull part of the blanket from the woman next to me. I wanted just enough to keep me from trembling and be able to go back to sleep. The woman noticed and yanked her cover away from me.

I chose to remain at the refugee camp until the following winter. Not much changed during my time there. I managed to acquire a bowl and a blanket. One night, as I lay frozen on my steel cot, I decided to crawl in next to an elderly woman, asleep on a bed close to me. She had a blanket and seemed to be sound asleep. I did not realize until the next morning that the woman was deceased. She just laid there, motionless. Nobody seemed to pay attention to her until the smell became too harsh to bear.

A Russian soldier noticed her corpse and examined her immediate surroundings. He found no papers nor pictures of identity. I yanked the lady's blanket as two brutal-looking men came to take her remains out. They threw a greyish blanket over her, grabbed her hands and feet, and carried her away. They buried her in the yard. As everyone else went about their business, I stood there wondering if similar, horrible circumstances could happen to my mother or dad.

There was nothing to look forward to except the thin soup the Russians brought to us every night. They would serve it at different times. Sometimes, we thought they had forgotten us. They hadn't forgotten. They wanted us to greet them with a little more fuss. We despised the Russians. We hated relying on them for our portion. The soup only served to keep us alive. The refugees had no strength left. Otherwise, some of us would have rebelled. We were just too weak to fight or rebel against them.

Winter came. Sometimes, it felt colder inside the hall than it did outside. Gradually, people noticed Christmas was approaching. We went with the flow of things. There was no calendar or clock to tell us the date, the day of the week, nor the time of day. The feeling of Christmas was in the air. We felt it. For me, it was my first Christmas away from home, and I was to spend it amongst strangers.

One night, I went for a walk around the streets outside the refugee camp. I put my blanket around me to keep warm. I felt blessed on this holy night. I could smell baked cake and the spicy smell of a roast. My mouth began to water. I could imagine the flavour of that tasty meal. I pictured my mother, in a stiff white apron, serving the Christmas supper. Then, my father, putting his arms around her waist, showing his appreciation. I gazed at the Christmas tree across the street. It reminded me of my childhood tree, which stood by the window with its candles and decorations during the holidays.

Unaware of my surroundings, I tried to get closer, to look at it from the side of the house. It felt like a magnet pulling me over the icy street. I didn't hear the Russian jeep turning the corner. It hit me, throwing me to the ground. I don't know how long I was unconscious.

The first thing I remember was touching my aching head. I could not see clearly. Things were moving in front of my eyes, but I could not pinpoint what it was. I tried to identify the person bending over me and holding my hand. I saw blond curly hair, parted on one side of the head and two friendly blue eyes. I thought he resembled my father. The pain felt like someone had put a dagger into my chest. I reached out to him as words rolled over my dry lips, "Dad, dad, you came back?"

My hands fell lifeless to my side, and I lost consciousness. When I awoke, I didn't feel groggy. However, my head still hurt badly. "She is awake." It was then that I recognized that friendly face with the two blue eyes and the blond curly hair. 'You are alright," said the blond man, "Only a bump on the head that will give you a headache for a while."

"Where am I? What happened?" I asked, realizing I was in a strange place. I knew I was not in a hospital. Perhaps, there were no more hospitals.

"My name is Vincent, and this is my home, for now. Perhaps, later when you are well enough to walk, you will recognize where you are."

"I was returning home after visiting a friend when I saw the Russian jeep hit you. It kept on moving. I picked you up from the street and carried you here. You must have heard the jeep coming around the corner," Mr. Jacobolski spoke in a friendly manner. His voice was deep but pleasant to my ears. He had been a Ukrainian soldier that managed to escape without becoming a prisoner to either side during the war. He mentioned he often wondered why he had fought.

Once I felt better, I told him what I was doing on the street so late. He cared for me as if I were a family member and invited me to come to him if ever I needed help. I did not share with him how much I needed help. Seeing as he could no longer help me, I chose not to share my needs and my pain with him.

I never returned to the previous refugee camp. Berlin had several abandoned movie theatres where the homeless lived. There, people like me fought for the garbage. We were content to find a piece of stale bread or a dry bone.

Along the way, I met several teenagers who had their own stories to tell. There was no one to teach us the right or wrong way of doing things. We stole because we were hungry. Some even committed murder and got away with it since there was no law, and there were no rights. The teaching of behavioural rulings was not a priority. Survival was.

In East Berlin, educated people, such as teachers, professors, engineers, and well-trained workers, were taken to Russia. Workers excavated the streetcar rails out of the ground. They sent them to Russia along with some of the underground trains. Perhaps, it was a form of payment the Germans owed to the Russians. I didn't understand why. When the factories started to produce again, ninety percent of the goods went to the Russians, while they left the other ten percent for the Germans.

Work was hard to come by, whether inside or outside the city. German prisoners were arriving from the east and west. Children, who had left their mothers, were now returning home. The German people who had left Berlin because of homelessness, due to bombings or escaping war zones came back. Men, with many years of hardship, were also appearing. They populated the refugee camps. Each one of us could relate to the other. There were so many people competing for work.

The influx consisted of people from all over Germany and Europe. Some refugees had nowhere to go, no place to live, no home to call home, no food, no shelter. Native Berliners, released prisoners of war, and German soldiers in their uniforms all stood next to me in front of the immigration building, which housed the unemployment office. It took days until I was lucky enough to get into the office. First, officers would listen to my case. Then, someone gave the final result, which was always, "We are sorry to have to turn you down." Perhaps, they were sorry, but the communist made the final decision, and that was, "No" coming from the back office.

At times, my home was a homeless shelter, and as unpleasant as it was, I felt I had nowhere else to go. There was no soup, no bread, no money, and no clothes. Like me, the same situation existed for many teenagers. I wondered if perhaps, some of us would become adults and have children. And if we did, would we be able to offer them better care than what we had. I often think back to what I once said and believed.

Every day presented a different challenge, so I ate out of the trash and begged for more food. Nothing hurts more than the pangs of hunger. My insides would turn, tear, and twitch with excruciating pain. I became pale, cold, weak and dizzy. To overcome this pain, one would eat anything, paper, even grass. One never saw a cat or dog twice. We would catch it, kill it and eat it. We, the teenagers, would trust anyone who mentioned candies and also food, and we offered our bodies since we had nothing else. Our very last treasures were our bodies and our pride. When someone would offer us food to fill our painful stomachs, we did not stop to think. We were free to be taken if someone wanted us.

Not only would the Russians take our bodies, but the Germans did as well—dispirited favours given for a piece of bread. There was no help to be found. They took everything from us, and in the end, they called us "the bad generation of our time." When I speak of "they" I refer to the luckier ones—the ones who had somewhere to call home and parents to guide them. Facing death today and waking tomorrow morning to face it all over again is something I sincerely do not wish for anyone else.

During my stay in one of the refugee camps in East Berlin, I met a girl, and we started talking about our backgrounds in Germany. When I told her I came from Landsberg-on da Wartha, the lady in the bed next to her asked, "Did I hear you say that you came from Landsberg?"

"Yes, "I answered, wondering why it was so special.

"I also am from Landsberg," she said in a sweet voice. "I have only been here in Berlin for a couple of days, and I wish I could go back to Landsberg."

"Why do you say that?" I asked, surprised that she would want to go back to the Russian caves.

"I would just like to. I worked for the Polish civilians, and I was able to make at least some money and could live wherever I wanted to. Show me a place that you could do that in Berlin?" she explained.

"Why don't you go back if there is a better way of living in Landsberg?" I responded sharply.

"I don't like making the trip by myself. It is better if two tried it. Besides, anything would be easier to swallow," she assured me. "I used to work with a woman, who told me that three of her sisters were taken away by the Russians, and she had not seen or heard from them since," she continued. "Would you know a Dora Schmidt?" she added.

"Do I know her?" I raised my voice. "She is my sister."

"What luck everybody else has," she made a wisecrack.

'Was Dora with anyone else? What I mean is, did Dora speak of my mother?"

The woman was unsure. "You said you would like someone to accompany you back to Landsberg. I will gladly come along, especially since you tell me I could find my mother and my sister there."

"Now, now, child, take it easy. As much as I would like someone to accompany me back to Landsberg, I didn't tell you the whole truth."

Fright filled my heart and senses as I listened to her every word. "See, kid. I only knew your sister for a couple of days. We were working together, and of course, we spoke of our families. I liked your sister, she is a good sport, but the next day she did not come back to work. At first, I thought she did not like the way the Polish people ordered her to work. In the evening, after work, I went to see her. She was alone, and I do not know where your mother was.

47

Perhaps, she was out looking for a doctor. Your sister is sick with diphtheria. I waited until late in the evening, trying to help her the best way I knew how. I left when someone else, maybe it was your mother, came to stay by her bedside."

There was a long silence between us. I was hoping she had more to offer. "What happened then? Did you ever go back to see her?"

"Yes, I did go back to her place just before I came to Berlin. She seemed to be in a coma, and her temperature was very high. I could tell by touching her forehead. She kept calling for Horst. Who is Horst?" the woman asked.

"Horst is her son," I answered. "Please go on."

"Well, I planned to come here. I bought food with my Polish money and got ready to leave for Berlin. One of the Polish neighbours offered to take care of her, and I went on my way," she finished.

It did not end the way I thought it would. However, I did understand that my sister was a stranger to this woman. Perhaps, I would have done the same thing had I been in her shoes. I might have left hoping someone else would take care of the situation. Now, I wanted to go back more than ever. Maybe it was not too late, and I could find Dora and my mother. I could help nurse my sister back to health. Nonetheless, I knew Dora would be pleased to see me.

I urged this lady to go back with me. "But you are only a child," she said. I would blame myself for the rest of my life should something happen to you while under my care."

"Nobody cares whether I am a child or not. Why should you? I have nothing more than you have, and I have to fight for things in the same manner you do. Now, will you come with me?

"I must say you are a hard cookie." She introduced herself to me, "My name is Hannelore, but you may call me Hannah."

"My name is Anneliese, and you may also call me Annie."

"And my name is Edeltraud. Can I join the party?" piped in the young girl who had been all ears during my conversation with Hannah. We called her Edda.

We discussed our plans. By morning, we decided to try to smuggle ourselves across the Russian border, wherever that was, and get into Poland. We knew Russia had placed a borderline in Frankfort on the Polish/German border, but the Russians still lived wherever they set foot. We, three women, had nothing to take with us, and that would make it easier for us to jump on the train. We hoped the train could take us far enough to the east.

We then had a slight delay in our plans. Hannah had a date with a Russian soldier and returned the following morning with food to fill our stomachs. We made our plans for departure and were ready to leave as soon as it got dark enough not to be seen by the Russians. In Lichtenberg, we climbed up the ladder of one of the boxcars on the train. We waited for hours until an engine pulled up in front of it. It was after midnight when our trip to the unknown started. Everything went well. The train only stopped once before we got to the Polish border. However, the worst part, I feared, was still to come.

I couldn't think of anything worse than what I had already experienced. My thoughts were already in Landsberg with my mother and sister. The train reached the border and stopped for inspection. During our trip, we had quietly stood on the iron ladder found outside of the boxcar. We did not speak a word to one another all this time. Then suddenly, Hannah's voice broke the silence.

"We better get off the ladder. When the train starts to roll again, we can run, and make a jump for it." So we did just as she told us to, and it was a good thing we followed her proposition. We saw Russians inspecting each boxcar from the long side and two short sides where we had just stood.

When the train blew the whistle and started to roll again, we sneakingly jumped back on it. Carefully, we listened to the call of the station master where the train stopped. From one of the stations, the master called out in Polish. Two Polish women got on the train. Their movement was suspicious, and I could not figure out why they had to do that. They were in their country, so I wondered why it was prohibited for them to ride on the boxcars. Then I realized they did not have to pay the fare this way. In these boxcars, they transported animals; no one was allowed inside. Besides, it was not legal to ride on one without paying.

It was quite a ride on the outside of a boxcar. Most people were malnourished, suffered from diarrhea, and many were nauseous. There were no washrooms. Also, we had to watch for posts and other accidentals on the side of the moving train. Plus, the ones on the side ladders had to beware of whatever might fall off the top. I was lucky to escape most injuries. However, I always had pain in my shoulder from a collision with a post while riding a railway car.

A couple of stations before Landsberg, screams were heard. I was not sure of who or where it had come. It happened so fast. I thought it could be one of us. We called each other's names, but we were all there. We concluded it must have been one of the Polish women that fell off. Wondering if she had been pushed or had fallen off, I realized one wrong move, and she could easily have lost her footing or her hold. She may have felt nauseous and gotten sick.

"Gorzow – Wartha – Gorzow," the station was called out by a Polish signalman or line keeper. Had I been by myself, I am sure I would have missed the station. It was a long time since I had last heard the name of my hometown called, and now it sounded strange to me. They had already changed the name.

"Come," Hannah said. "We are here at last." Hannah and I knew every wrinkle in the train station. As we got off the train, we tried not to be seen by anyone. Edda, who had never been in Landsberg before, stumbled over almost every stone under her feet. We walked along the bulwark, which meant a short cut for us, which nobody used since Landsberg had become Polish. Besides, it was still dark out.

We stood close to one another, and when we were about five hundred feet from the bridge, which we had to cross, we stopped to review our plans on how we would cross the bridge. We knew they guarded both sides, but often only the Russians kept watch.

Hannah had a pass to show that she lived in Landsberg and worked for the Polish people. Edda and I needed something to show but had nothing. Then I remembered that in my knickers, I had a pocket in which I kept the only identity I had. I once obtained this from the doctor, stating that I was under a doctor's care in Landsberg. There was no date on this piece of paper.

"That will do," Hannah said hopefully. Now, we had to figure something out for Edda. We brainstormed every possible scenario. Still, our plans did not look good. Hannah yelled out, "I got it! I got it and why not? It is only a thought, but perhaps it could work. Edda, you are the smallest person here, and I can hide you under my raincoat. With the belt, I can tie us together into one. Of course, I will be quite fat, but it's not like I am the only fat woman around." I know it sounds amusing, but I never heard of such an idea from anyone in all my life. We were at the border and had to take our chances. As far as Hannah was concerned, when silly thoughts came, that was the thing to do.

"If we get started before dawn breaks, I am sure we can fool the Russians on the bridge," she added. I know Hannah asked, but Edda did not like to take that kind of chance. They argued. Hannah suggested Edda should perhaps go back to Berlin instead of making it hard for the rest of us. I felt the same way as Edda, who wanted to continue to Gorzow, but I did not dare say a word to stand up for her. We all agreed to try.

"Good girl," Hannah replied. She knew she could get through to Edda. It was too dark for me to see the two women joined into one. Now they started to exercise to keep the same steps at all times. It was a dangerous plan we wanted to see through, even though I could only make out a little of Hannah's figure. Despite it, later, the very thought made me laugh so hard my stomach hurt. I could not remember the last time I had allowed myself to laugh like that.

We had to keep quiet even though we did not see anyone around. It was possible someone could have been nearby. Once Hannah was satisfied with Edda, we walked very close to the bridge until Edda went under Hannah's raincoat.

"Let me do the talking," Hannah commanded in a low voice. My heart was bouncing so hard I felt it would come leaping out of my throat. Then I heard the Russian call "STOP." It made me jump with fear. I reached for Hannah's hand. I didn't want her to feel how frightened I was. I could not help myself.

"Don't worry about a thing. Once he sees my size, he likely will think twice before he starts to tangle with me." I tried to encourage myself, although Hannah was also afraid. The Russian kept asking something of which I understood very little, but Hannah answered. I then figured out he was asking for our identification cards. Hannah told him that we had to work in town and were trying to get home. After Hannah showed him her pass, he didn't ask to see mine. With the light shining from the flames of the matches, he tried to read the pass. As far as he was concerned, that was enough.

"Quite a big load you have to carry with you?" He asked Hannah. Once again, I thought I would die from fear. I was sure he would frisk Hannah. But he only meant her figure. "Yes," Hannah replied quickly.

We all hoped it would be as easy to go in the other way. And we were lucky. After all those shocking moments and the cold sweat, we decided once over the bridge that we could use a rest. We sat down on the sidewalk before continuing on our journey.

# CHAPTER SIX

# Hope and Despair

*H*annah would lead us to where she had last seen my sister. After a few hours of walking we reached the place where my sister was recuperating. From far away I could hear a rooster calling and the morning starting to brighten.

Dora had survived, and the fever was gone. She was feeling more energetic. Only weakness lingered. She cried with joy when she saw me, for she was not expecting to see me and certainly not in Landsberg. It became a joke when we told Dora how we crossed the bridge. Even the Polish woman that took care of Dora had to laugh. Of course, no one wanted to believe us, but in the end, it was funny.

Dora was still too weak to go out and work. I felt that it was up to me now to make the best by finding a job. Polish people had moved everywhere in the city; in the stores and homes which were not in a pile of rubble. The stores and businesses were operating. It was not hard for Hannah, Edda and I to find work. We were the cheapest help available. Germans were still living in Landsberg, but there were fewer left.

Of course, we didn't work in any one place for very long, nor did we stay together. Sometimes the stores would get robbed, or the pay was too low. We had to work to buy the things we needed.

In Berlin, the same German money was still the currency. When I had first left Landsberg, the coins and bills, especially from the banks, laid all over the city streets and sidewalks. I had hoped to find enough to take with me when I returned to Berlin. I knew I couldn't and didn't want to stay in Landsberg for the rest of my life. Others must have had the same idea as there was not a coin in view. Before my leaving, no one had been interested in the money, not even me. At that time, one could not buy anything in Landsberg with it, and I, like others, saw no use for it.

While I was in Berlin, many visitors had passed in Gorzow. Dora explained that it was said over seven thousand Italians now lived in the Wilhelm's Siedelung (A siedelung is a German word meaning settlement, a small village where many family houses are situated in a quiet location.). Hannah and Edda liked having Italian boyfriends. "At least they are clean, and above all, they are human beings the same as we are," Hannah observed, acting like a woman who liked to flirt but forgot how to do it. I was only fifteen, and my sister did not allow me to go to the siedelung without supervision. Once in a while, Dora let me accompany her and her boyfriend to the siedelung. Dora knew how I enjoyed their singing and dancing.

Hannah was right. The Italians were just like us, clean and friendly. But like any other place and time, the Russians came to control the Italians the same as they did with the Germans. The only difference was that the Russians gave the Italians a ration of lard, flour, and sometimes potatoes to cook with their meals. The Italians appeared pleased to share their food with us, even if we came uninvited for lunch or supper.

As the summer of 1946 was coming to an end, the Russians arranged transportation to send the Italians home. With their luggage at hand, they happily went to the station to embark on their travels back home. Many had lived in parts of Germany during the war, but most of them were prisoners of war. Like a caravan, the dark-haired Italians moved slowly through the streets. My sister, walking along by his side, escorted her boyfriend, to the station. All the while, Hannah, Edda and I followed their friends with laughter and songs through the streets of Gorzow.

While the Italians did not like to part with their belongings, the Russians insisted that they store them in the goods car. Being worried about contradicting the Russians, the Italians arranged everything as planned. Everything was safely stored, and when the last goodbye was said, the train started to roll away. We watched as it increased its speed. The boxcar, in which their goods were stored, did not follow the train. It did not surprise me that the Russians did not let the Italians take their belongings with them. It was now too late for them to get off the train and reclaim their luggage. The Russians had a flair for stealing from the poor.

Dora, Hannah, Edda and I stood there waiting to see how the Russians would go about claiming the cargo. "Now I have seen everything," my sister commented, almost surprised at the Russians' sly plan. "That's communism for you," Hannah mocked. "Take all and leave nothing to the ones who have nothing to spare."

I decided long before that I would never become a communist no matter the consequences. It was a disgrace to hear some saying they were joining the communist party. I felt sorry for them. I sensed that they did not know what they were getting themselves into. My slogan was "live and let live." If someone wanted to join the communist party, I was indifferent.

I witnessed so many atrocities and disturbing attitudes from people during that period in time that I concluded: each one lived in a way to self-survive. No one said I had to live in the same fashion. I and only I was master of my mind, but of course, I was not the master of my life. Perhaps one day, the sun would shine for me again and for other struggling teenagers. I was very thankful to have found my sister. Little did I know how short-lived my situation would be.

When summer ended, and the fall brought cooler nights, Dora decided to go back to Berlin to look for our mother. Dora and my mother had tried to get to Berlin in the past. They didn't make it because the guards watched the bridge in Frankfurt too closely. It was impossible to swim across the river, yet some tried it, and we never knew if they made it or not. Hannah wanted to stay in Gorzow, but Edda and I wanted to return to Berlin. I wanted to follow Dora and accompany Edda, who wanted to return since Gorzow was not her hometown. In the end, Hannah decided she did not want to stay behind by herself. Therefore, she joined the group to plan our return trip.

Dora took me aside that evening, announcing that she had heard that a Doctor had returned to the old neighbourhood. She believed that it might be Doctor Friedlander. The same doctor whom the Nazis had taken when they had burned down the Jewish Temple. "He might have news of our father or our Uncle Henri. We can not leave without verifying what he might know of our father's fate." Before we would leave what had been our home town, we needed to make inquiries.

Our return to the old neighbourhood where we had lived before the war was agonizing for us both. We began our search in a small drug store on our very own street. We were told that it would be the place to verify on the chance that he had started a small clinic of some kind. Doctors being in high demand, he had not been hard to find. As we knocked on the door of his living quarters, we were surprised to find him thin and aged. He recognized Dora as soon as she introduced herself and invited us to come in and sit down. "We are hoping to find news of our father," she began. The doctor raised his hand and just stared at the floor for a minute and began to speak.

"We travelled on the train together to the death camp. When we arrived, we were silenced by the shouting of the guards with guard dogs. All of us were frozen in fear. They came in pushing and shoving, leading us out with their guns. There was so much fear; we all felt this was the end. Some of us followed, some of the prisoners ran. Your father ran. They sent the dogs after them. It was dark. There were gunshots. I never saw or heard of your father after this."

At this moment, tears came, but time stood still. I could not listen to what was said. I could not function. My sister was still speaking with Doctor Friedlander. The shock of this moment was so intense;

I had a hard time concentrating on what was happening around me. When it came time to leave, I got up and followed my sister. My only memory was following my sister to the refugee camp. We never spoke of it after that evening.

The same way we came to Gorzow was the same way we left our hometown again. Whether or not I see Landsberg once more, I thought to myself, was to be seen. That night, we waited for the train to stop by the station. We were waiting, from late in the afternoon, so that we would have no trouble getting over the bridge. There existed a curfew now; no one was to be on the streets by nightfall. We managed to stay close together and leave by boxcar. Before reaching the border, we found ourselves in the company of a Russian soldier. He came around to where we were, and in a broken German, he demanded our jewelry and money. We told him we did not have anything to show. We would gladly have given our belongings in fear of what he may have done to us should we refuse.

The Russian soldier stood beside Dora. He must have felt her hand and found that she was still wearing her wedding band. It was dark, and I could not see his face. All I could see was his slim silhouette. He demanded that she take the ring off and hand it over to him. For many years, my sister had not removed the ring from her finger. She found that her finger had swollen. Therefore, she fought in an attempt to remove the band, which did not come off.

"I will be back," the Russian said, "and I hope you have the ring off by then. If not, I will cut the finger off to get it." By the tone of his voice, we knew he meant what he said. While he was gone, Dora tried hard to get the ring off her finger. She licked her finger over and over again, but it would not slip off.

The train had stopped, and we were on the Polish border when the Russian soldier returned and asked for the ring.

"I can't get the ring off my finger," a nervous Dora answered. He tried himself and found that she was not lying and made us get off the train. There, the soldier searched each person, but could not find anything of value. He ordered us to get back on the train. When the train started rolling again, he jumped off and pulled my sister with him. It was so unexpected that we did not react fast enough. Without delay, I stood up and screamed in the night. But no one heard or cared except the two girls that were with me. They were just as stunned as I was. I wanted to jump, but Hannah and Edda held me back. The two hung on to me as if they knew I would jump after my sister.

It would have cost me my life. I would have blindly jumped and probably have killed myself. Only later, after Hannah, Edda, and I had returned to the homeless shelter, did I lay in the straw-covered bed and begin to wonder how much help I could have been to my sister if I had jumped. What could I possibly have gained if I had made the jump safely? It did not matter now; I had to move on.

I thought of the words Mrs. Schweitzer once said to me. "We had six years of good living during the war. We didn't starve, and we had a home. Now that the war is over, the suffering begins."

I came back to Berlin and, for the second time, found the city with little law for protection. It was winter, and again, I stood, waiting in front of the refugee camps and homeless shelters. We tried to keep our shelter warm, but that seemed impossible to do. The search for firewood or anything that would keep the oven warm went on for most of the day.

My world became a wilderness where I was living like a wild animal chased by savage hunters. Each day, I would find them waiting in several different disguises. In the winter, I met the hunter, masked under the hat of sickness and cold. In the heat of summer, the hunter became a savage man. It was hard to refuse a small piece of bread from a man, perhaps the only meal for the day. The man used this form of temptation to charm his prey. We had no parents to guide us, no home to go to, and no money to buy food. We were easily trapped.

Today, it was one monster and the next day, we faced another. No one wanted us any longer than one night for what they called their fun. The Russians said, "Drink, Frauline, Drink." The Germans would also take us for their pleasures, although we were not theirs to take. They would say, "Why should the Russians have all the fun and not us. We have suffered even if we lost the war." We were hungry, cold, frightened and lonely children, fighting to see another day. We may have been young, but there were no laws to protect us. We were not even given respect from the elders.

Some of the girls had soldier boyfriends. The girls were chased from the barracks but often returned, as hunger was more potent than the soldiers' threats. I found these girls "lucky" because they found the courage to offer their bodies for a piece of bread or some cigarettes.

I used my courage to search for food in the garbage cans and to beg. If I saw a chance to, I would steal it. It took a lot of courage to do that. No matter how often I did either one, I always felt ashamed, but hunger pushes the boundaries of pride and decency. My search for food, from one day to the next, brought me to the East end of Berlin. I walked several miles in one day.

In the summer, the sky was my roof and the stars my guiding light. I slept in what was called "hause-flurs." They were house halls or in parks. In the winter, I slept in what we called the hause-keller, which was a house cellar. These places became my shelter for the nights when I found myself too far from the homeless shelters or the cover of refugee camps. As I passed the unemployment building, I would put in a claim for a job. I filled out some forms just to have made the effort of looking, not expecting anything. I was living on the streets, stealing, offering myself for any goods I could sell, and selling it on the black market. I was always hungry, and I would do anything for a piece of bread.

One day, checking the employment office for the possibility of a job, I made my way to the office of lost persons and continued my quest to find my mother and my sisters. The details and questions were numerous. They asked details of the last days with my family, aspects of their appearance, like the colour of eyes and hair, their weight and height, the clothes they wore, and their age. They asked what happened at the time we were separated, "You will hear from us," said the clerk as he finished my interview, "check with us every few months."

It took a long time for results. Most were looking for someone they had lost or looking for work. Organizations were in chaos and hope was at a minimum. The outlook was terrible for finding a job. Eventually, I heard from a clerk of a possibility. I did not care what it was, I had no training to speak of, and I felt ready for anything.

My group of teenagers stuck together, and we made many friendships. One place we gathered almost daily was the coffee shop at the railway station.

I checked in periodically on Mrs. Schweitzer. One day, my sister Lotte appeared. Mrs. Schweitzer had directed her to find me as they had met one day. Although we were happy to see each other, a particular bond was missing. I was sixteen now and not all that innocent. But still, she was the adult, being eight years my senior. She offered her help in finding my mother. She sent me a man who she thought could help me. The man found me too young for him; he admitted he had given her money to have me. That was the kind of help my sister was giving me. She never invited me to her home, but she did have an apartment.

CHAPTER SEVEN

# First Job, First Home

*F*inally, someone gave me a job. I was to work an elevator in a Jeep factory, taken over by the Russians. There were rules to follow, and I needed proper clothes. My dress was showing signs of disintegration, and my shoes had holes in them. The woman in charge of recruiting employees met with me. "Now it is up to you to agree on the things we asked of you," she said, taking a cloak and a pair of boots and shoes from the open closet and placing the items on her desk.

"The manufacturer's cost is two hundred and fifty east marks for the cloak, and that is the price we are willing to sell it to you. The boots and shoes are fifty east marks." Together they total three hundred and fifty east marks.

"It sounds like a lot of money," I replied. I was in no position to pay that sum of money as I had just started to work. And who knew what tomorrow would bring. "Well," she said coolly, 'it will be fifty east marks a month until you pay the sum in full. I could arrange for you to take the cloak and the shoes today," Miss Flaken encouraged.

"Of course, we have no guarantee but the good words of your co-workers. I already made some enquiries. Your reputation is good. We like to help young people like you when we can, of course," she added politely. She knew how much the work, the cloak and shoes meant to me. She also knew that I would do almost anything she would ask of me. After a moment of reflection, she added, "If you would like to join the F.D.J."[1]

She looked into my eyes and patiently waited for my answer. I needed the cloak and the shoes to keep my job, or else things would look sombre for me again. I agreed to the terms and signed the contract to pay the fifty east marks per month. In a large black book where the Free German Youth had written their names, I added mine under theirs in small letters, "Anneliese Möwis." (Note: one East Mark was approximately one American Penny. Therefore, 50 East Mark was 50 cents.)

On my way to the refugee camp, I figured my wage and how much I could pay per month to pay it off quicker. I did not pay rent while living at the refugee camp. Reflecting this, I realized it was not the best deal for my dollar. I was pleased with my purchase but not with the situation.

1. The F.D.J was founded in January 1936 through the merger of the Young Communist League of Germany, Socialist Youth League of Germany and the Socialist Workers Youth. It was an underground anti-fascist movement to oppose Hitler and the Nazi Party's rule during the war.

- Reference found on Wikipedia

Like most people in East Berlin, I wanted to trust our rulers, but I had seen so many devastating things since the liberation from the Russians. It is no wonder I was against communism. I was in need, and by joining the F.D.J. party, my needs were met. On the other hand, I had to pay back more than I could afford, but it was a necessity for me. I could now cover my worn clothes with the cloak, and no one would know how poor I was.

The day before Christmas Eve, each worker received a bottle of vodka and a can of mashed corn. In the cafeteria, we got an extra piece of rye bread, an addition to our daily meal. That night, they welcomed everyone to a party. Cake and coffee were served, and there was a floor show put on by the F.D.J. I met with them in the afternoon to plan the evening with the F.D.J., but when the evening came, I didn't attend the party. Earlier that day, I spoke to the girls in the factory, asking what they were wearing to the party. Each one of the girls, a little more fortunate than I, had a dress to wear and enough life left in them to enjoy them. I sacrificed the cake and coffee, which I had longed for two weeks prior, and a meal, which I could not get at the refugee camp, not even for Christmas. I still had enough pride and knew I would look out of line had I gone to the party. Instead, I chose to stay at the camp.

I didn't even have a piece of soap to wash my face or my smelly body, no comb to untangle my hair. I commonly used my fingers to straighten them out. I sat on my bed with my neighbour, and we opened the can of mashed corn with a pair of scissors. After a few small cuts on our fingers, we finally got the can open. I was famished, but by the first taste of the corn, I spat it out on the floor. It had a bad smell when we first opened it, and the lid of the can was black as well as the side walls. I did not want to open the vodka, as I hoped to sell it on the black market. My friend called me a poor sport. I thought it was too much vodka for just the two of us. Opening the bottle, I invited everyone to enjoy it with us. Our empty stomachs reacted to even a half-cup full. Soon we were all singing Christmas carols, and it was not yet Christmas Eve. Many of us would have given everything we owned to forget the hunger and pain, if only for a moment. We had no time off for holidays. Sunday was the only day of rest.

A week later, on the way to the cafeteria for my lunch, after the New Year, I ran into Miss Flaken. "Hello, dear! Did you have a happy New Year?" she asked.

"Yes, thank you! "I replied.

"We missed you at the Christmas party. Why didn't you come?"

I was not sure that I should tell her why, but I felt I had to. "I had no clothes to wear."

"Well," she said, "if you had only told me about it, I am sure we would have found a way to help you out of your little problem."

"I am sorry, but I did not want to be more trouble to you than I am now," I answered.

"It would have been no trouble at all. On the contrary, we are here to help anyone who needs it," she assured me. As she was leaving, she reminded me of the meeting that evening.

I was pleased she did not ask more questions. I did not have any intention of attending the meeting, as I did not understand their purpose. I knew too well that I had signed my name to this obligation in the black book, but I could not convince myself to attend these meetings unless they were planning a social event.

Before I sat down at the table with my fellow workers to eat my lunch, I took a look at the blackboard to see where and when the meeting would be. Before finding what I was looking for, I saw a sign which read: One large room for rent. Suitable for one or two working people. It was signed by Joseph Walter, Steel plant B #1. I quickly ate my rye bread and ran to find the person who had put up this notice.

I had to hurry in case someone else was quicker than I. Past the big main building, stood the Steel plant B #1, where I entered. I found it filled with noise and heat. To the first man that passed me, I asked where I could find Mr. Walter. The man pointed to the north end of the plant. "In front of those big ovens," he said. When I reached the man I thought to be Mr. Walter, he stepped toward a table and wrote something on a piece of paper.

"Excuse me, please. Are you Mr. Walter?" I asked.

"Yes, what about it," he answered in a deep voice.

"I saw the sign on the blackboard, which mentions that you have a room to rent," I replied.

His eyes scanned over me as he asked, "How many of you are there?"

I didn't quite comprehend his question, and so he repeated it. "How many girls would you like to share the room with you?"

"There is no one else," I said, trembling.

"The room is a very large one, and it is too much rent to be carried by just one girl," he shouted.

He started to walk back to the ovens under his care and got busy feeding them with fuel. I couldn't leave; I had to try harder to make him rent me the room. Some of the other men stopped for a moment and looked over at us. I was embarrassed because he spoke to me in a harsh manner. I was somehow used to people turning me down, but he was someone that I would not cross yet. I ran behind him, hoping he would hear me.

"Perhaps, if I saw the room, I might later get someone to share it with me. I wish you would not give up on me so soon. Besides, it is January 9th today, and it is my birthday." I spoke fast and hoped I could reach him with my plea.

"No harm done in looking at it," he responded. "I just live around the corner of the plant on Wilhelminhof Street," he instructed. "I will be home anytime after five-thirty this evening." "Thank you, thank you very much," I happily said as I turned on my heels to walk out.

At five o'clock, the plant siren blew, and everyone walked through the big Iron Gate, along the driveway towards the streets. Today, I was in a hurry. I thought all afternoon how different it would be now. Though I didn't have the room yet, I could still dream.

Most of the workers had a family at home. They lived poorly, but they were together, and that was appreciated. I had forgotten that I had a birthday today. Too much had happened through this last year as a refugee. I reminded myself that it was January 9th, 1948, and I was 17 years old, but I gave my age as 19. I wondered what it would be like in another 15 years. Would I still be a refugee? Would I be married by then and have a dozen children around me to call me Mom? Only God knew the answers to all my questions. I also liked being nineteen (even though I was seventeen), and able to go into movie houses, which younger patrons were prohibited from attending.

"You miss one month's rent, and out you go," he firmly said while smiling at me.

In the room, there was a dining room table. On the south side of the room stood a chesterfield instead of a bed, two chairs and an old fashion closet cabinet. I had to admit it was a big room that not even a few furniture pieces could make it look smaller. There were no longer any glass windows. Instead, the windows, stuffed with cardboard, hardly kept the cold out. Any average person would have refused to take the room for two reasons. The first being the high priced rent, and the second, being the fire material needed to keep this place warm enough to be comfortable. Unfortunately, we had a season called winter; otherwise, it would not have mattered as much.

Regardless, I took the room. It was clean and mine to live in, to dream and hope for better days to come. That night I felt like a queen sitting on her throne while lying on my chesterfield. I thought of finding someone with whom to share the rent and expenses. With that thought in mind, I fell asleep. At seven-thirty, Mrs. Walter woke me; it was time to get ready for work. I had not forgotten the refugee camps as they were part of me, and in my mind, I still considered myself a refugee. Registered with the main branch in Koepenick, I was authorized for a room and a ration card, thus allowing me to live this way.

Koepenick laid South- East of Berlin, where the Russians had their Kommandanture (command post), and they controlled most of the work in and around East Berlin. From there, came the final word whether or not the person could stay in Berlin to continue working at the factory. As I had experienced so many times before, I was frequently turned away from a job. I felt I was capable of doing more than just wait around in a refugee camp for something like this to come my way. I had to try and try again to keep my job.

I needed to give up my refugee status for my ration card and a place to stay. "Come back tomorrow," the officer said. The next day, I returned and the next and the next. Finally, I met a lady that could help me. She was a pleasant enough woman. Pleading my case, I explained how important this job meant to me. I explained that I had lost my family in Landsberg and that while working here, I was able to get permission to be registered to stay and obtain a ration card. Following this pleasant meeting, the woman left the room for a short time. She returned with papers signed by a senior officer. "There is one more thing," she shared, handing me the documents. "If at any time you leave the plan we just agreed on, you automatically lose all authority to stay in East Berlin or have access to a ration card." With this bit of advice, I left the office too happy to worry about what could happen. Besides, I never did like to look at the darker side of life. Happiness and worries occurred so rapidly that I could cry one minute and laugh the next.

At that moment, I was happy, but worries took over when I thought of the bill I had with the F.D.J. and the rent that was due within the next few days. I did not know who to pay first. If I did not pay my rent on time, I would lose the apartment. Besides, this was my first month. Yet, if I did not pay the bill for my clothes, they would come and take my coat and shoes. On top of all this, I had to buy my food from the ration card. There would no longer be the free watered-down soup.

I saw myself helpless in many ways, not knowing what to do first.

In the end, I had no other solutions left to solve my dilemma. I came to a decision where I would attend the meetings, and perhaps that way, I could talk my way out of paying my bill that month. And so, I paid my rent instead and promised the F.D.J. to pay a little more the month after.

I had a ration card now, but the food ration was never enough to make it from one week to the next. I was always hungry. I found new ways of getting extra food from the black market. It was very active in East Berlin. A small loaf of bread cost five east marks, and five buns were the same price. I remember a can of meat, the contents of which no one knew anything about, except perhaps the packer; I had found short animal hairs and shavings of bone in the can, and it cost about 18 east marks. Coffee mixed with peat filler cost 50 east marks for a pound. Sugar and white flour were available at a pound for 30 east marks. These were high prices for anyone trying to survive.

Before I realized what happened to my money, it was all gone and still, I was hungry. It was challenging to live in the refugee camp and find enough food in the garbage cans. Any chance I had, I was checking the garbage from the Russian army compound, but they would always chase us away. It was now hard to find enough food away from them and, at the same time, continue to work. I visited the black market and spent any extra marks there.

During the next month, I found a roommate. Margaret was quite happy with the arrangement, and we became friends for a while. We decided, at one point, to give our ration cards to Mrs. Walters. With this, she would make it possible for all of us to get enough to eat each day. The lady agreed to that, but I'll always remember the shock of it when we came home soon after to find our meal on the table. We knew it would be small, and neither one of us wanted to look under the cover. I picked up the lid to find what a daily portion was. I stared at two potatoes, a teaspoon of margarine and two slices of bread. My friend and I looked at each other and started to laugh. It was not a laugh of joy but two insane persons. Yes! We had to be crazy to live the kind of life we had to live during this period in time. Of course, it was not quite all we had to eat from our daily ration. There were still two more slices of rye bread to count for lunch.

No matter how hard we tried to work, eating less to get sufficient energy seemed impossible. "I only know of one solution," Margaret said. "We should find ourselves some boyfriends. I certainly will," she stated.

In the following week, I told her that I found myself a boyfriend and asked her how I could get some food from him. "Well," she said, "when I mentioned a boyfriend, I certainly wasn't thinking of a German boyfriend, my dear. They rather prefer that you give them food, but you sure would not get anything from them."

All the while she spoke, I could sense how disappointed she was, but I did not let her know I understood. "You know him, I am sure. His name is Guenther Heine. He is also in the F.D.J."

"I do not care who you choose as friends, but don't come crying on my shoulders, I have enough of my problems to deal with," she replied quite bluntly.

It was only natural for a girl my age to want a boyfriend. I didn't want anything from them. Besides, I rather liked this young man. He told me that he had longed for me to attend the Christmas party. Not knowing where I lived, he could not find me.

On our first official date, he took me out to a theatre. They presented a play of how the Russians came into East Germany and how they helped the German people and brought back happiness after the Nazi power. Nothing, absolutely nothing, could be compared with the things I saw and had experienced myself. It was all a pack of lies. I became bored and frustrated before the play was over. I laid my head on his shoulders, and he gently pushed me away.

After the play, we had our first and final row. We had reached the door to where I lived when he broke the silence. "I am sorry I pushed you away. I really didn't mean to, but I was enjoying the play very much and found it to be fascinating. I didn't realize what I was doing. I apologize."

Maybe he meant what he said, but I did not care for him any longer, and we wished each other goodbye and good luck. It still bothered me days after Guenther and I had broken off our relationship. I also wondered how he could find this play fascinating, so much so that he became someone with no feelings of tenderness. I wondered where he was when the Russians deliberated the Germans from the Nazis. Were the Russians different in Berlin than in Landsberg?

Perhaps, the Russian army had cooled off when the war in Berlin came to an end. While in Landsberg, when I faced them, the war was still on, and many of the wounded Russian soldiers who came from the front were treated in Landsberg. On the other hand, I do not want to influence my beliefs on others. Nor can I expect that everyone in East Berlin or East Germany had seen the Russians in the same way I did.

The following Sunday afternoon, Margaret asked me if I would like to go with her to see an old friend of hers. Having nothing better to do, I agreed to come along. Music and loud singing in Russian, welcomed us, as we walked over the ruins into a part of a house that was still standing. In the basement, in the quarters where she told me her friend lived, to our surprise, we found Russians eating and drinking vodka. Frightened, I asked her to go in first. I would wait outside until she returned to get me. Instead, she pushed me inside in front of her towards the basement. Among the five Russian soldiers sat an older woman and a younger girl. Margaret received a warm welcome at the door as she made the introductions.

The Russians introduced themselves. Before I could figure out what was happening, I sat at the table with all of the others. They offered me food with a glass of vodka. Shyly I refused, but they insisted, and I gave in. The men were joking but being a bit crude. At sundown, the older woman tried to get the Russians to leave. She had no further use for them. They had come for the meal, but the Russian soldiers had plans of their own. The music had stopped, the food was gone, and the soldiers were drunk. The older woman whose name I have forgotten tried to protect her daughter, but two of the Russians did not like that. They wanted the girl, and it became a horrible scene. The Russians pulled the girl to the floor, and then the older women pulled her back towards her. That went on until someone suggested we all go out for a walk.

Three Russians pulled Margaret and me out of the basement. After walking for about fifteen minutes, we entered a cemetery with tombstones. The cemetery and the streets were quiet, and there was not a soul around. It was quite dark by then. No one was about to stop the scene that was unfolding. The Russians were holding us by our arms. There was a bad feeling in the air.

Margaret sat down on the green grass; there was a lovely arrangement of trees surrounding the stones. The Russians began to argue who was going to get who first. One of the men sat down beside Margaret, but jumped up real fast and started yelling. "Moi chasy, moi chasy", but I could not figure out what he was saying. He had lost his watch, and he was yelling," My watch, my watch," as he searched through his coat and pockets for his watch. Margaret got up fast and came to me, whispering," I stole his watch. I was going to make him look for it on me." But the soldier was getting upset and accused both of us of stealing. The Russian pulled out his gun and demanded we hand it over to him or he would shoot both of us.

It is the right place to die, I thought to myself. At least our bodies do not have to be carried far. The darkness had crept upon us, and it was getting quite eerie. We feared the worse. The two other men were beginning to look down on the ground where he had been sitting. They tried to calm him down by explaining he might have lost it in the basement after our meal. Margaret and I took the opportunity to run. I headed for the trees. Margaret was zigzagging around the headstones. It did not take long for one of them to catch Margaret and brought her back to the small clearing. Two of them were yelling and kicking her.

The one with the gun had started running after me. I had on my finer boots with a heel, and I kicked him hard in the shin. He let go of me long enough for me to hide in the evergreen trees. I laid down on my belly in a crevice. The ground was very uneven, and it was too dark to see. I stopped breathing and did not move while he stood nearby, listening for sounds of movement. I was horrified, frozen in fear. He began rummaging around as he stepped on my shoulder but kept walking. My black jacket helped to keep me in hiding as I hid my blond hair with my arms. I thought he would just bend down and drag me out as he stood by me, waiting. I could hear Margaret yelling as she was being beaten and raped.

I wanted to save myself, and I blamed her for getting us in this mess. I figured that they would come back for me when the others settled down. I did not move from my hiding place until everything was quiet again, and the men had left. I quietly got up and waited for the morning light to leave the cemetery. Margaret had dressed when I saw her, and she had decided to wait until morning to leave also. We left together but angry at each other. I told her if she wanted to visit friends, she could go on her own.

A week after that, we had to attend another meeting with the F.D.J. They were organizing another social evening of dancing. This time, I really wanted to participate. So, I took the opportunity to buy a second-hand dress from my landlady. I had become dedicated to my work and would never arrive late or take any days off. Margaret was planning to attend, as well. She was starting to be more serious with her boyfriend. I was not a good dancer, but I had met people my age and we were all planning to have a good time. I left alone and early, still feeling out of place. Margaret told me her boyfriend would take her home.

When I arrived home that night, things were not right in the apartment. Something made me feel uneasy. Someone had been in and rummaged through our possessions. Our most precious belonging was our food. As I looked in our cupboard, it was clear that someone had taken all of it. I looked in several places to see what else was missing. We did not own anything else valuable. My only worry at this time was how Margaret would take it. Would she believe what I needed to report?

Immediately, when she arrived with her boyfriend, I told her our place was burglarized and what I thought had happened. I could not believe how this upset her so much. She began yelling and started accusing me, "You liar," she yelled. "It is you. You ate my bread, and you're trying to tell me we had it stolen. Someone came in here and ate all the bread. It's hard to trust you lately. You stand by while I get beaten and raped, and you eat all the bread as soon as you're alone in here!"

I was astounded at her reaction. Trust is a big thing, and it's hard to trust anyone when you never have enough to eat. Perhaps, I would have felt the same way, but things started to turn bitter. It hurt to hear all this, but it would not have hurt so badly if her boyfriend had not been standing there. I wondered what he thought of the whole thing.

Things started to escalate into an argument. We raised our voices and tempers flared. Margaret's boyfriend was furious as he growled. I felt a sting across my cheek. I felt my eyes water from the blow to my face. "How dare you steal food from honest, hardworking people?" He grabbed my shoulders and started shaking me, and I flopped around like a rag doll. I was whining by then and begging him to stop and let me go. "I'll show you to steal," as he resumed slapping my face until it was red, burning and hot. The landlord and his wife came through the door to stop the commotion, but still, he threw me to the floor, and as I got up, pushed me on the sofa and my head resonated against the wall. I thought he was aiming to kill me.

Margaret began explaining to the owners what I had supposedly done. I was too weak to respond. Tears were running down my face, and I had a hard time explaining. Neither was going to help me. By their faces, they believed every word she was saying. I asked Margaret to move; the trust and friendship were over. She had a hard time looking me in the face. I had taken the apartment first and believed I had the right to ask her to leave. But she had no place to go and neither did I.

It took one week to make a complete investigation of my person. By disturbing the peaceful life I had been living in the last two months, the wheel of destruction was upon me. The following Wednesday, I had a visit by a security guard from my workplace. He insisted I return my cloak and boots for neglecting to make payments. I returned to work the next day, where they told me I was no longer needed. Having neglected attendance at the youth meetings was inexcusable. I lost my job, my home, my clothes and my ration card. I was back out on the street.

# CHAPTER EIGHT

# Refuge with the Nuns

*A*refuge with the Catholic Nuns was a desperate attempt at leaving the hard life. As I came to their door, I was invited in by a nun that smiled and said, "Follow me. I will bring you to our Mother." I did not know their customs, nor was I familiar with their Superior. As we reached the door to Mother Superior's office, the nun knocked on the door, stepped in and I followed. "This young girl would like to speak to you, Mother Superior," she announced and left the room.

"Thank you, Sister Martha," she added. "Welcome to the house of God," she replied with a warm smile. Hungry for warmth, love, and food, my evil side responded as there is no other explanation for the lies that followed. Then the question came:" So you want to become a nun?"

"Yes," I answered without looking into her face.

"Are you certain about this?" Mother asked.

"Yes, of course, I am certain," I continued lying.

"I presume you are Catholic, and you still attend mass?" And here, my heart fell as the few times I had ever attended services was with my friend Rosa Schultz when I was back home. I wished at this time that I had been raised in the Catholic faith. I remember asking my parents to let me become a Catholic like Rosa, but they had been against it. I did, however, continue to attend mass with her whenever the chance arose.

"We cannot accept you if you are not Catholic. We have to turn many young girls away because of this." I managed to bluff my way in. I remembered being with Rosa, the day she had done her first communion, and I spoke to her about confessing my sins and taking the Holy Communion. I talked to her of the old priest, Father Lucas, that I had met with Rosa years ago in Landsberg. I also knew that all they offered would have been refused to me if the truth was known.

I had a feeling that Mother Superior did not believe me, but that was that, and I would stay until she turned me out into the street. The first thing she directed me to was a bath and fresh clothes. She gave me a long black dress to wear and told me to tie up my hair under a black veil. For the first meal, I was assigned a seat, and everything was under quiet strictness. All the nuns stood with head bowed and hands clasped in prayers before the simple but wholesome meal. I had a feeling of safety and direction.

The first few nights were cold, and I could not warm up underneath my blanket. In the beginning, I shared a bedroom with three other nuns, until a bed became available in the dormitory where a group of girls slept in a big room. Girls my age slept in rows of beds very much like in the refugee camps. But here everything was spotless; the air smelled fresh, and all speaking was in hushed tones. We were the helpers, and the nuns gave our assignments. I also had to learn a series of prayers.

The day began with prayers after the first signal of a bell. Then a group of five nuns would enter singing loudly. Being nearest to the door, I would jump out of bed as if a hornet had bitten me. After prayers and breakfast, they assigned different duties.

My first assignment was with the kinder-garden children. Most were orphans. They had lots of needs, and I felt impatient with them. By 10 am, we would be directed to the chapel again and led through more prayers and singing. In the days I was with the Catholic nuns, I was required to work in the kitchen, preparing meals and washing dishes. After a few mishaps, I transferred to the laundry, washing, hanging and ironing clothes. The breaks in the day were prayers, prayers and more prayers, and singing. After the first few weeks, the novelty wore out.

After prayers one morning, I crossed myself. Shivers ran through my body as I prayed for forgiveness and guidance. I left the chapel without waiting for the other girls. I crept along the corridor, crying and leaning against the wall. I made my way to the Mother Superior's office. Now, I decided it was time to confess. I could not live like this.

Mother Superior understood fully; the temptation to an offering such as the Convent was a relief compared to the awful pains of hunger. She offered for me to stay and study to become a Catholic nun. Unfortunately, it felt like a prison to me. It felt like the walls were closing in on me, and I couldn't stand it. I could not live with the sisters day after day, who would know I entered these walls with lies. I walked for hours after my release, punishing myself for having been untruthful. With all my experience, I had rekindled my faith in God. In there, it had been a different world of purity. Unfortunately, I chose the outside world of misery and evil.

# CHAPTER NINE

# A Russian house

*I* tried my luck at the employment office again. I felt elated inside, and I was satisfied to try any avenue. I was directed to a home in the French quarters where I found a small house with a garden—the name of the street I have since forgotten. Behind the house was a small barn-like garage, but the garden gate was closed, and I rang the bell under the name J. Stranalskow. A tall woman with black hair opened the gate and asked me what I wanted. I told her that I was sent to work for her as a housekeeper. She did not seem pleased at all. The expressions on her face startled me, though I was hoping the position had not been filled yet.

Expressing her disproval of me, she mentioned wishing for a stronger girl. "Oh, I just look small," I replied, "but I can do the work of two," I assured her. She led me to the kitchen, where I met her husband, who was sitting at the table drinking coffee. I felt uneasy and wanted to turn around and run back to the refugee camp or at least to a place where I could cry. But I knew I had to be strong if I wanted the job.

"I am sorry you disapprove of me," I tried to convince them that I was willing to work. "Well, I can't wait any longer for anybody else to come. You will have to do," Mr. Stranalskow replied angrily. I couldn't figure out if he was upset with the agency that had sent me or with me.

Frau Stranalskow offered me a cup of coffee, but it was the first time in my life that I had coffee, and I knew by the bitter taste that I believed I would never like coffee. I drank it regardless, as the warmth felt good in my empty stomach. It was almost evening when I reached the Stranalskow's home, and I had missed supper. Therefore, I went to my room and had nothing but the coffee in my stomach.

The linen was snow white and fresh, the room small but clean; nonetheless, it only served as a place to sleep. After making my bed each morning, I did not return until it was bedtime.

In the morning, Mrs. Stranalskow showed me my duties around the home. She ran a small grocery store while her husband helped her to build the counters and repair the floors. In the afternoon, they would leave me alone to complete my duties while she went to the back of the store to check that everything was the way she wanted it.

During the following days and weeks that I was with the Stranalskows, both would be gone from eight o'clock in the morning till after nightfall each day. Sometimes, they returned after eight or nine o'clock at night.

When they left, I did the morning dishes, swept and scrubbed every floor in the house, dusted the furniture and got the supper ready for the evening. I also did the weekly wash and the ironing. After Mr. and Mrs. Stranalskow had their supper, I had mine in the kitchen. My meals were always rationed, and from the day I came, they made it clear that I had to go by ration cards. Sometimes, Mr. Stranalskow let me use his bicycle to go to the camp. I told them I would work the same as two, and they certainly took me at my word.

At Christmas, the Stranalskows killed a sheep they had, and my Christmas present from them was a piece of sheep's ears with potatoes and gravy. I was grateful for this humble supper. In the refugee camp, I would not have had such a feast.

Every second Thursday, the Stranalskows went to a show in the Russian canteen or a theatre with their friends. By accident, I found a photo of the couple with a Russian colonel lifting his glass of alcohol. On the back of the picture, I believe he had written, "From my dear comrades." It was no wonder they could go to shows and theatres, eat and drink and temporarily forget their problems. Out in the many apartments, homes and refugee camps, the people were hungry. I felt ashamed to have taken a piece of bread from people who belonged to the "communists." Nice home or not, I planned to leave without telling them about it. Little did I know that Mr. Stranalskow would speed it up for me. I had planned to leave on a Thursday when the two were out. As it turned out, I found myself trapped. Mrs. Stranalskow went out on Thursday night. I was in bed, planning for another opportunity where I would leave while they were out. Without knocking, Mr. Stranalskow pushed his way into my bedroom.

"Are you comfortable?" he asked, using a fatherly tone. Frightened and startled by his appearance, I pulled the covers higher to my neck.

"I am fine, thank you," I replied politely though my voice gave away my fear.

"Don't be frightened," he said as he walked closer, then sat on my bed beside me. "I just wanted to see if you were comfortable. I would like to do things for you, but you must understand my wife would not like it, as she hates Germans."

He continued to speak as his hands worked their way under the covers. He bent his head, wanting to kiss me. I did not know his wife hated Germans, and perhaps, it was he who hated them. He always had a drink and was rarely seen without a glass of vodka in his hands. However, this night, I noticed that he did not have one. His breath and his hands smelled of tobacco.

"I will give you anything if you are nice to me." He seemed sure of himself. "You see, my wife is a sick woman," he continued. "It is hard for me to see someone young and fresh like you around our home, just a reach away."

I hung on to my blankets as he continued talking. I refused to kiss him, but he then held my arms with his hands as his wet lips reached for mine. I turned my head, trying to avoid him.

"Let's forget the matter," he said after he was unsuccessful. Have a drink with me, and I promise never to touch you again. He saw I did not want to get out of bed. I would have hidden, had there been a place for me to hide.

"Don't get up. I will bring a bottle and glasses for us." He left the bedroom door open so that he could keep an eye on me, should I try to escape. Before I could plan my escape or say anything, he was back with the bottle of vodka and two tall glasses. He filled the glasses to the very top. "Let's drink to the future," he said. "Let's drink to Communism and may it grow and always be strong and promising.

It was the most vodka I ever had consumed. My head started to spin, and everything stopped. I was feeling so light, free of all my sorrows and fears.

To me, he was the perfect Communist. I never trusted them, but I never dreamt that one of them would sit at my bedside and wait patiently. I hoped I was wrong about them. I hoped what I heard and what I saw myself were only dreams, bad dreams. On this horrible night, I lost my faith in God and everyone else. For the first time in my life, I met the beast in humanity, who believed the glory of Communism. No matter how I fought to free myself from his hands, he had such a brutal force. It felt as though he was breaking every bone in my body. Digging my nails deep in his skin didn't discourage him. He had bleeding scratches on his face and arms. He only pulled himself into a deeper furry for not being satisfied. Finally, he simmered down, for he must have felt the pain from the deep scrapes on his face.

He staggered for a minute when he lifted his heavy body from mine. Then, he walked out of the room. When he came back, he had seen his face in a mirror. I could tell by the anger and hate in his eyes. He hit me across the face with all his might. "That's for the face you gave me. Now get out of my house," he yelled.

I thought I had lost my mind and all my teeth. It did not hurt me as much as his forced advances had done. I expect he must have been worried about his actions and that his wife would question him, and I, therefore, understood why he wanted me gone. Afraid of his own shadow, he yelled at me: "You are worthless, you whore. Now get out of here." I got dressed as quickly as I could. He had opened the door to freedom and of course, I did not want to lose one more minute in his house.

I had to admit to myself I was drunk. I was having trouble putting my shoes on. Each time I felt for them, they somehow jumped away from me. Finally, I took my time to put them on, and I ran out of the house. "I will tell my wife that we had a whore in our house, and she will understand!" I heard him yell behind me.

I staggered along the dark street until I reached Main Street in Spandau, which is a French sector. This street would lead me to the subway train. I think I would have preferred he shot me down like a dog instead of having to face the world in my condition. I felt like a wounded animal along the street, and as I fell to the ground, I had an awful time of getting back up on my feet. I had to run as far as I possibly could away from the house, which I never will forget.

Even the main street was empty. As empty as I felt inside, I did not notice anyone through my troubled eyes. Then, I saw two French soldiers with their German girls walking in the opposite direction. They were laughing loudly and happily as they watched me stagger along the street. The four of them waited for me to pass. Perhaps, I looked odd to them, as drunks usually are. They seemed to find me comical. I, however, did not share their humour. My broken heart was still processing what had happened, and tears were still pouring down my face. "Perhaps one of the soldiers got the better of her and kicked her out on the street," I heard one of them say in broken German. Yes, I was kicked out and landed on the street, like a pest. I fell on the sidewalk and could not get up. I cried myself to sleep there and awoke at daylight. It took me a few minutes to realize what had happened to me and to relive the occurrences of the night before.

Ashamed, dirty and bloodstained, I wanted to die. How could anyone be so cold-blooded? People who passed by me looked at me with expressions of disgust. I felt I was the only one from the refugee camp who had no protection and attracted so much trouble for myself. I was so alone, no one to turn to for guidance and encouragement. Such was the reason why I so wanted my life to end.

.

# CHAPTER TEN

# Lotte

*A*shamed to face anyone in the refugee camp, I made my way to the railway station, hoping I wouldn't meet anyone there. The railway stations in Germany became hangouts for the black market dealers and for anyone who had nowhere else to go. That was in addition to the ones who had to travel and were waiting for the train. Those who travelled were few.

The waiting room was a big hall with a food counter; only it had no food to sell. It was closed.

I sat at one of the tables with my eyes fixed on the tabletop. I put my head on my arms and cried myself to sleep. I do not know how long I remained in this position, but I heard a familiar voice that woke me. To my surprise, my sister Lotte sat in front of me.

LOTTE

"I noticed the bloodstains on your arms and legs," she said. "Are you OK?" I broke out in tears from embarrassment and disgrace, surprised that she showed some sympathy. I was relieved to be able to share with her what had happened. I needed to unload. I felt I was becoming crazy. The tears were rolling down my face as I recounted the previous night's horrific event.

I felt better after sharing my story with Lotte, who comforted me. She tried to cheer me up, offering to meet me at the station every Wednesday. She gave me some news about our family. She had been in touch with Dora. Dora knew where mother was, but she could not tell me much more other than she had her two boys with her, Horst and Roberto. It felt good to meet her again. We parted ways promising to meet the following Wednesday.

It was pouring rain outside, and the skies showed no signs of clearing up. My mood seemed to be worse during the period of rainy weather. With nowhere to go, I hung around street corners and at the railway station. I often stayed in an abandoned movie house where a variety of people loitered around. This is where I reacquainted myself with Vincent Jacobolski. We became a couple. He would look out for me, and I looked out for him. We would share whatever we made from the black market, food and clothes. I could barely stand the ghastly smell of a blend of tobacco, filthy clothes and body odours in the big hall. Ordinarily, the theatre would fill up with people, most of them sleeping. I would find a seat and keep the seat beside me for him. He would do the same for me. I preferred the old theatre, off the street and out of the cold. During the day, I would sleep when I could. All kinds of things took place here: prostitution, black marketing, fighting for seats, etc.

In the months that followed, I searched for work, but I would often vomit during the day. My face became pale until I was unrecognizable. My eyes were bulging, showing fear. There were dark circles around them. One day I saw myself in a mirror that stood in an abandoned store. My body was extremely thin, all skin and bones. Looking at my image, I saw a face that was so pale and sad. I could not believe the sight of me, Anneliese.

I was once happy, friendly, and smiling. I felt full of mystery and part of the neighbourhood children, but of course, all that seemed so very long ago. Now my image reflected things I never imagined possible. I felt misjudged, indecent, misled, frightened by horror, assaulted and, most of all, full of fear. It defines the living nightmare of my life. Then one day, a friend of Vincent came to announce that there had been a raid from the Russian police at the Railway station. Gunshots were fired, and Vincent was killed. Our relationship had not lasted very long, but we had deeply relied on each other. Vincent had been my first love.

As we had done during the past, I met Lotte on Wednesdays. My mother was willing to have me visit, she announced and Dora would come with me. I was so excited and full of hope. Dora was married, and her last name was Asmosen. Her old friend Elizabeth would also come. My mother lived with a Russian couple. She had been hired to take care of a disabled woman, living an hour north of West Berlin. We had to travel by train and walk along the railway tracks to get there.

We visited for one afternoon. The reception was a cold one. Although my mother seemed happy enough to see us arrive, she made it clear that I could not stay there with her. I had to remain on my own. The depression I felt from the turn of events was unbearable. It was nice to visit, but no help was forthcoming. I was on my own.

On my return, I found a job working for a woman, Mrs. Muller, who owned a bakery. In the initial interview, I asked her for Wednesday afternoon off, and she had declined, offering me Sundays off instead. Lotte was waiting for me at the station that following week. I could hardly wait to tell her about my new job.

"Guess what!" I blurted out. "Beats me," replied Lotte. "You have a new job?" "Yes, I do. I explained I work for a couple who own a bakery called Koepenick, a German bakery, they have no children, and the work is just like a "Kinder spiel," (child's game). Lotte was asking a lot of questions, even small details. As I was leaving, she asked if we could still meet on Wednesday afternoons. "No," I replied. Wednesday is a bad day now since I am expected at work. Why not make it Sunday afternoon instead? She agreed and away I went.

I got up at seven in the morning and had breakfast. After Mrs. Muller and her mother-in-law had their breakfast earlier, they would leave to go to the bakery, which opened to suit their customers. Miss Mantel, the store helper, came three evenings a week. She usually came first to the kitchen, where she knew I would save her a cup of coffee. My room was on the second floor, which was in the attic. I had a large bed, big feather pillows and a blanket. After four days with the Muellers, I received two lovely dresses and four white aprons from them. I felt like a Queen.

As I cleaned the Muller's bedroom, I could not help myself from looking in the closet. It was part of my job to put away clothes. Looking through her things, I couldn't see the damage to only satisfy my curiosity. She had lovely clothes. For almost every dress, she had a pair of shoes to match. I wondered how she had managed to save those from the Russians. All this and a little more, I shared with Lotte on Sunday.

"At least you are not starving anymore," voiced Lotte. I had not realized she was scheming a coup. For our next visit, I had saved some bread from my breakfast and dinner to bring her. I usually would not include bread with my dinner, but now I accepted it with every meal. I also added half a loaf of bread that I took from the box. The following week, Mrs. Muller called me in the guest room, where I was seldom allowed to enter. "Anneliese," she started, "Did you take the bread out of the bread box?" Ashamed of being caught, I felt the blood rushing to my face.

"Yes, I took the bread," I replied timidly.

"Why did you do that?" she asked, troubled. "Is it because you were still hungry and took it for yourself?" "No," I responded slowly, "I am not hungry anymore, but I know people who still are."

"You do know that is stealing," Mrs. Muller answered. Her tone presented some severity but not unkindly.

"Yes," I replied.

"Well, then, I will have to punish you! You will not leave the house at any time, including Sunday afternoon until I tell you, you can resume your day off." Mrs. Muller explained. She reminded me a lot of the way my father would speak to me. I liked her a lot more after that day.

The first and second Sunday passed, but still, Mrs. Muller had continued my punishment. On the next Wednesday afternoon, Lotte came to see me. The Muller's were busy in the store. Therefore, I had no fear that someone would come to the kitchen and see us. "I was worried," said Lotte, "when you did not appear at the station." After talking a while, I invited her to see where I lived and how I worked for a good family. Lotte was surprised and pointed to all the things she would like to have one day.

"How long before you are finished with your work?" questioned Lotte.

"It is five o'clock now," I answered. "There is at least two more hours before suppertime. I do the supper then clean up, only then am I finished. Tonight the Muller's will stay up later because of all the stamps from the ration cards that need to be transferred on paper." It is quite a long process.

"Perhaps I can come back a little later, said Lotte. "I am sure Mrs. Muller would not object to my visiting you." Unnoticed, she left the house.

At supper time, I asked Mrs. Muller if she objected to my having a guest. She looked at me with a sympathetic stare, without complaining.

"Who is your house guest," she asked smilingly, "a man?" I recognized her insinuations.

"No," I quickly corrected. "It is my sister who is visiting," I blushed.

"It is alright," she replied. "We are very busy this evening," she said, and her mother agreed.

It was nine, and I had given up on Lotte's visit. When she arrived, she gave some lame excuse as to why she was late. Nonetheless, I was happy to greet her. At approximately ten-thirty, she asked if she could have a glass of water. Like a good hostess, I went down to the kitchen. On my way down, I thought that I could ask Mrs.

Muller for a couple of glasses of hot milk instead. It was the first time I had company, and I didn't know my limits as to how I should go about receiving my guest.

It was dark and cold outside, and I was sure that Lotte had not seen a glass of hot milk for a long time. I went from the room along the corridor to the bakery store. Behind the store was a little room where I knew I would find Mrs. Muller. I knocked on the door and then entered.

"Yes, Anneliese," Mrs. Muller said, looking up at me, and without waiting for an answer, she continued, "Has your house guest left?" From the tone of her voice, I decided not to ask for the milk. Instead, I asked if it was alright for Lotte to stay until eleven.

"If you can find your way out of bed in the morning without complaint, I think it would be alright. However, I might remind you that it is ten-thirty."

"While you are here, Anneliese," she continued as she raised her eyes from her work and looking up. "Are you not feeling well these days? You seem paler in the mornings from when you first came." Although she seemed to speak out of concern, I felt intimidated; I bent my head looking at my hands, hoping to find a way to leave. "I didn't mean to worry you," I said out of concern at the possibility of losing my job. Mrs. Muller was still examining me as I asked if I could leave now.

"Yes, you may go and enjoy yourself. Besides, a girl of your age should have many friends and perhaps go out for walks. You are too much in the house all the time. Of course, you were punished, but I mean, before your punishment, you only went out on Sunday afternoons. That is not enough. Anneliese," she added, "you don't have to fear for your job. You are a good worker and an honest, steady person. If you like it here, we like you too, but you have to look after your health. Let me know if anything is bothering you."

I noticed that my clothes were getting too tight on me, but I blamed the regular meals I had been having. The paleness Mrs. Muller spoke of could have come from all the sweet things Hanz, the old baker, kept for me. Perhaps, I should stop eating the desserts if they made me ill. Besides, these things cause me to put on weight. I forgot how hungry I had been before I came here. At that time, I had neither good food nor sweets to eat. I put it out of my mind as I filled a couple of glasses with water and returned to my room upstairs to visit with Lotte.

While I was gone, my sister had kept busy. Lotte had been plotting to steal from the Mullers. She had emptied Mrs. Muller's closet and threw her things out of a window. She proceeded to include me in her plans. We could sell whatever we did not want to keep on the black market, but we had to hurry. She had planned this out for some time. She had returned that evening with a sleigh to steal their belongings. After the sled had been filled, she left with it. I stayed to pick up my things, but I never made it out in time.

As I went back in to gather my personal belongings, Mrs. Muller confronted me wanting to know what was happening. Mrs. Muller's face expressed anger and horror as we stood in my room. I couldn't find any words to answer. I sat in a corner and could not move from the chair. I could not escape, but Lotte managed to leave without me safely. Mrs. Muller stormed out of my room, and then I heard the door slam downstairs as the house stood still.

The police arrived with Mrs. Muller a half-hour later. They arrested me, knowing Lotte had been to the house, and so the search continued for her. I wondered what I would tell the police. In fear and angry at myself, I searched for a suitable excuse. In the end, my story may have sounded unbelievable, but it was the truth. Sitting on the same chair, feeling very uncomfortable, ashamed, I became very angry with myself. I had allowed Lotte to convince me to act in such a deceitful manner. I could not direct the police to Lotte as I did not know where she lived.

I later learnt that Lotte had managed to hide the stolen goods and sell them on the black market. I realized that I was causing this entire disturbance to people who gave me a job and a place to stay and to other people that I hardly knew. I kept blaming myself for being so ungrateful for the events that followed.

By the time I got to the police station, Lotte was there looking out for herself. She was strutting around as if she was part of the police staff. They led me to an interrogation room. I thought she was going to help me, but she only helped herself. The way she was acting, she looked like she was turning against me. She was blaming me for the robbery, but she had all the goods. She seemed so quaint and sure of herself that everyone believed her. And I never saw her again after this encounter. She was free, and I was locked in a prison cell.

# CHAPTER ELEVEN

# Prison

*F*or the first time in my life, I sat behind iron bars for something I felt was a setup. Others, whom I knew, were guilty of other crimes, like Margaret Hoffmann, the girl who stole from me and got away with it. She had taken everything I owned and made me lose my apartment. The police never found her. How fast they came this time compared to when I needed them in the past. I was so confused; things were happening too fast. I barely felt the hard bed under me and couldn't think straight, paralyzed in mind and body.

In the morning, I was awakened by the warden and ordered to wash up. They gave me prison clothes to change in. Soon after, one of the guards came along the corridor and handed me a cup of tea and a piece of stale rye bread through a small window opening in the door. I felt like my good days were over.

After breakfast, I was guided to the warden's office in the main building. I was told to repeat my statement and said the same story as the previous night. A detective was present; he smoked heavily and amused himself at blowing the smoke in my face. The warden was not pleased with my recollection.

"You must admit that all the details of the robbery point directly at you," he yelled. "I have been patient with you." After two hours of questioning, the warden ordered me to sign a statement but prevented me from reading it. I refused to sign it. At some point, the detective came too close to me, and I heard my hair sizzle. "For now, you will go back to your cell." Everything felt so hopeless.

Eight days passed, and every night I was taken to the same German detective. Repeatedly, the same questions were asked: "Where did you come from? Where are your parents? Why was your father taken to the concentration camp? Where was Lotte, and where did you hide the goods?" To my utmost surprise, he also asked who the father of my baby was. These last words hit me like a ton of bricks. I suddenly felt weak and asked what he meant by that. He revealed I was pregnant and I did not even know it.

During that time, I was repeatedly slapped in the face, told I was lying and that I had fabricated my story. After some time, I would return to my cell. I had a hard time falling asleep and felt a lot of pain and mental anguish. My mind was wondering what would happen to me now that I realized that I was pregnant.

Less food was offered to me during that week, and I grew weaker each day. In the summer of 1949, I signed a statement that I never read. Shortly after that, I stood trial for robbery. The Jury was merciful because I was pregnant. I pleaded guilty, and my penalty was three months in jail.

I shared my three months sentence with five other girls. My jail mates were from the city of Berlin, and we all found no Justice. The department of justice was nothing else but a bunch of cutthroats. If we had money or anything worthwhile, we would no longer be in jail. One of the girls made a statement: "How come we only hear of simple class people being jailed and mishandled but not the big shots; the ones who smuggled coffee and wine by the trainload?" She was right, and I knew that.

Anita was fourteen and sentenced to one year for picking pockets. Renate was twelve and sentenced to two months for prostitution. The oldest, Wanda, had been charged with robbery and sentenced to ten months. She was eighteen and promised herself that she was going to have a real ball. She had robbed a Russian transport carrying vodka. "Half the bottles were broken, and the other ones, we drank," she told me laughing. "You should have seen the lot of us having a blast."

"Alexander, my boyfriend is in jail with three of his friends. I don't know yet how much time he and the rest of our gang got," showing distress for her friends. "When they found us," she continued, "we were so drunk and played ball with the policemen. We sang the whole night through until we were separated." She kept laughing so loudly that the warden knocked on the door and demanded silence at once.

In the corner bed sat Marilyn, quiet and without paying much attention to the rest of us. It took me a long time to find her name. "She prefers not to mix with the other girls," Renate replied, after noticing me trying to become acquainted with Marilyn. And it did take a while before she shared with us.

During the week, the routine was always dull. We were awakened at seven by a loud bell. We had to be out of bed and dressed quickly. Water to wash our hands and face was never enough for all of us girls.

At eight o'clock in the morning, breakfast was handed to us through the little window in the door. Mostly, we had coffee and stale bread. Other times it was tea and stale bread. The coffee and tea had no taste at all, and sometimes we could not tell if it was one or the other. At eight-thirty in the morning, our cells were opened. We all had to march into the jail yard for our daily exercise. During this time, the girls exchanged the latest gossip. Some girls heard rumours that the warden was a lesbian. They accused that she had tried to get one of the girls to be nice to her. The warden may have been a lesbian, but I would not have recognized one from the other.

I knew men by now, but I feared lesbians. In my last few days in prison, I became uncomfortable with the warden, who was showing concern about my future. In an interview on the final day of my imprisonment, she offered, "I will give you my home address, and you can come and stay with me as long as you need, or until you can find somewhere else to go." Avoiding facing her, feeling shame, I replied, "No, thank you very much. I will manage on my own." Yes, I told myself, I will manage somehow, but how, I did not know. I had made no plans, as they never came through.

Not long after, we heard the ring of a bell. It was the signal to go and see the social worker. I was relieved to leave the warden's presence; she kept looking at me as if she wanted to eat me alive.

We both entered the social worker's office. After a few words with the social worker, she asked the warden to leave us.

"You are free now, Anneliese. Don't let this happen again. I would not like to see you back here. In my view, I like you; you are a clean and fresh person. You have a warm personality, but you trust the wrong people. My name is Miss Vanderberden, by the way." While she spoke, she stood up from the chair and came slowly behind me. I felt her hand on my shoulder, being friendly and understanding. No one believed me when I would tell them that I had not robbed Mrs. Muller.

I was released and full of fear about returning to my previous life. I was a bit grateful that I had been locked up. Sometimes, I wished I could have stayed. At least there was a bed to sleep at night and clothes to wear, regular food, routine, exercises and warmth. Now I faced freedom, back in the life of nightmares, refugee camps, cold, hunger and fear. I wondered at the time how it was in the concentration camps. I heard talk in the train station but not until later in my journey from East and West Germany, did I realize the pain, the real suffering of the poor, the sick and the starved.

Several times, I have watched people digging large holes and filling them with bodies. I felt the despair in people every day of my miserable life. Just making it alive from one day to the next was a chore; eating bread in peace was hard. I was fighting for every piece of food I could find. The Germans had lost the war, and it was taking a long time to get things organized. Why did a child have to pay?

It was not me alone anymore. I was pregnant. I wanted to stop fighting and die. No one would miss me, or feel sorry for me. All these hopeless thoughts went through my mind, but I still had a will to live. I had to get married and have my child. I wanted this so much that it all felt like food to my soul to keep me alive. I had desires that things would get easier. It had to get better. I did not know how it could get worse.

# CHAPTER TWELVE

# Crossing to West Germany

One gray, rainy evening, I walked towards the Alexander subway station, where people walked about without purpose. People of all ages were walking very slowly. No one seemed in a hurry. Far from the entrance, along the long subway corridor, I saw a group of people, some standing, and some sitting bent on their heels. I walked towards them. I got close enough to hear their voices, and I overheard their conversation. "We could take the train to the end of the Russian border and try to cross from there," I heard a woman's voice. I could not make out her face.

I walked past them as slowly as I possibly could and just far enough that I could see the group of people and their every move. I had a feeling that they planned to cross the border, and I decided I would be among them, only, I didn't know how yet. I needed time to think things through and chose a corner to plan my strategy if I wanted to follow them.

One hour passed, and the group of people had not made their move yet. I had no idea how I could fit into their plan. I thought of every possible scenario to integrate myself into the group. One reflection kept coming back to mind again and again. Abandonment by my mother and two sisters was the deciding factor for me to leave the country. I had to ask them to take me along. Just simply ask, and I was sure they would not refuse me. Besides, why should they?

I made up my mind and walked over to the group. I didn't want to cause any suspicion to others around in the subway. I pulled a woman aside by her coat sleeve. "Excuse me," I started, "I couldn't help overhearing that all of you want to cross the border this evening. Would you please allow me to come along with you?" She quite abruptly cut me off. "You want to cross the border?" she continued quite sarcastically. "Child, in your condition, you wouldn't walk more than a mile." She then turned to face the group. I did not realize my pregnancy might be a problem.

"We would do better to lower our voices, as the girl behind me just asked if she could cross the Russian border with us," I heard the woman warn the group. Slowly I went back to my corner. It was a foolish thought to anticipate that they would consent to allow me to cross with them from the East zone. I contemplated finding more possibilities that would help me approach the border crossing with them.

Even if they would consider letting me come along, I still had no money for travelling. I heard them plan that they would take the train up to the Russian border and then walk across. I wasn't giving up. Just listening to the plans and excitement, I felt no pain of any kind, even the hunger pains had eased.

I was sure now that I would follow them wherever they went. I wondered why they waited so long to make a move. I was eager to get started on this journey. Then it dawned on me as I recalled the border crossing from Berlin to Landsberg. We had chosen a time when it was good and dark and realized they too would wait until the darkness was just right for their plans.

I don't know what time it was when the group of people, one after another, started to leave. I had never seen this group before. They did not look familiar to me; nonetheless, I was determined to follow them from a distance. I felt that some members of the group heading for the railway had noticed me, but no one attempted to stop or chase me away. When we left the station, it was dark, and I had a hard time staying close. When we reached the railway tracks, I knew that this journey was going to be menacing. I decided to move closer to the group, so much so that I could almost touch one of them.

We were a group ranging from young children to seniors. It was still raining and getting colder. Few were dressed for the weather, and most of them were shivering. We stood hidden in the ditch along the railway track, waiting and hoping for a train. Then we saw the steam engine, and luckily, it moved to attach the car that we hoped it would pull.

What would I have done had I been alone? I don't think that I would have had the motivation to wait there, in the dark, by myself, for a train to bring me to the border. I had the courage, but by myself, I would have been less motivated. We sure needed the courage to smuggle ourselves on the train, and when we reached the station, before the Russian border in "Oschersleben," the rain was at a downpour. It was very uncomfortable for me as we slipped off the top of the wagon train. From there, we continued to walk towards the station.

Mrs. Ecklemann, the woman in charge of the group, was a thin, tall lady, in her thirties. She asked many people there about the border crossing. One man, who came from the west side of the border, told her in a low voice that the Russians kept a very close watch for anyone crossing. In the past few months, thousands had crossed over to West Germany. He also told her that, for a hundred East marks per person, he would bring us safely to the other side of the border. I understood now what his business was. I couldn't help wondering how much he would have made from us if we had agreed to his offer.

We were all tense and afraid. It made it harder with each moment that passed. I would have tried over and over again to get to the west side. It was the first time crossing for most of us. Mrs. Ecklemann asked many questions. The stories we heard from both sides of the border were very discouraging.

At one point, Mrs. Ecklemann asked if anyone had the time. The group guessed approximately three o'clock in the morning. As time was passing quickly, she advised us to be ready. She then announced, "We best be on our way, or we will be picked up in the morning by the Russians and land in the jailhouse." I had spent time in their filthy jailhouse and did not want to return.

I was cold and wet, and the rain kept pouring. I couldn't help wondering how Mrs. Ecklemann would go about crossing the border. I was sure that I wouldn't recognize one edge of the border from the other, not only because it was pitch black. However, a young boy who seemed to know the way well enough guided us away from the railway tracks towards a farmer's field. We walked along ditches filled ankle-high with water. We all followed him, but Mrs. Ecklemann still gave the order to lie down or move on when she felt the need.

I found it very difficult to walk. After a while, I could no longer differentiate if I was walking in water or if I even had shoes on my feet. From afar, we heard a Russian calling, "Stop! Stop!" A few shots echoed back from where we laid. I crawled in cold water in fear and pain. I was happy to be able to follow without causing unnecessary trouble. The Russian voices grew louder and closer. We all had to be as quiet as possible. Because of the rain, we were unable to judge just how close the Russians were. But we made it across.

Later in the morning, wet, cold and hungry, we reached the safe ground in Helmsteadt. There were no police, nor watchmen, to sent us back to the Russian zone. To eat and sleep in a room or refugee camps, we needed money, which was something I did not have. Refugees could find shelter in a large barn for the day and night if they wanted to stay and rest. I was too weak and too sick to go much further. Therefore, I stopped for the night.

There were many farms in the surrounding area, and like many times before, I went around to them and begged for food. I knocked on a farmer's door and asked for a sandwich or a glass of water. I would only take what the farmers gave, and it was enough to take away my hunger pains.

How different it felt here on the other side of the border. I did not know how well the people lived, but there was a sudden feeling of freedom. I did not remember exactly where I was, but I continued walking for miles by myself. My feet just didn't want to carry me further, and the day was coming to an end.

It was time for me to find shelter for the night. I couldn't find a refugee camp or a place where someone could spend the night. By this time, I was also starving and had to find something to eat. I knocked on a door where it happened to be a minister's home. A middle-aged man in a dark blue suit opened the door and asked what he could do for me. I could hardly talk to him, but I could smell the coffee and fresh-baked bread. I had been walking all day without food. And now, hours later, I was famished.

"I am a refugee, sir," I stuttered. He waited for my request. "I need shelter for the night, sir, I am cold and hungry. I come from a long journey."

"I am sorry, girl. I can offer you neither shelter nor food, and also we have more than enough refugees in this small town of ours. No, I have nothing for you, nothing at all. Be on your way now," he ordered.

He spoke in haste and with an angry tone in his voice. I could feel his eyes examining me and the coldness in his words. I was positive that if I begged him, convinced him that I had nowhere to go, he would reconsider.

"Perhaps I could have a glass of water," I pleaded.

"Martha," the man called along the corridor. A small girl with black hair and friendly eyes came out of a room down the hall. "Yes, Reverend Guenther," she humbly answered. Her black dress and her white apron revealed that she was a servant. "Give the girl a glass of water and send her away." I could tell the minister did not want to see me here any further.

I followed the girl into the kitchen. She filled me a glass of water but poured it back out. She then filled the glass with milk, which I happily accepted and gulped down fast. She then offered me another, and I drank this one a little slower. While I drank my milk, the maid asked me where I was from and to where I was planning to continue my journey. I explained to her where I came from two days prior, that I had crossed the border with others, and once we reached the west side, everyone had gone their own way.

She commented on how she admired my courage. "Even if this is not the best place to work, I could never be so brave. I, too, am a refugee from Ostpreussen. My mother stays on a farm with my younger sister and brother. People around here do not speak well of refugees. They more or less treat them like some kind of outcasts. I do not know why, but I feel it, as do others around here." She broke up the conversation rather abruptly, as she noticed the preacher appearing in the doorway.

"You are still here," he uttered in an unfriendly manner. I almost hated him for his poor attitude towards me. He asked the maid for a cup of coffee, and while she got busy with pouring the coffee, the man turned to me and asked in a demeaning tone, "Where is your husband?" Ashamed, I did not answer him. "You do have a father for the child that you will give birth to soon," he continued? He was now looking directly in my eyes. I informed him: "I do not have a husband, nor did the child I carry under my heart have a father, he was killed." I spoke honestly and no longer had a fear of him as his cold grey eyes did not impress me for his lack of compassion.

"Well," he said, "another refugee who couldn't stay on the right path of life. While we clergymen preach our gospel, but what does it bring us?" While he spoke in a disgusted manner, he picked up his cup of coffee and walked out of the kitchen. He had spoken the mighty word. I thanked the girl for her kindness and went on my way.

Along the dark streets, I cried about the harshness of some people and because I was lonely and afraid. I cried, for I had lost my way. I couldn't see where I was going; I may have turned back to Schoenberg. I would not know until daybreak, and that was a long time later. I walked and walked until I collapsed.

When I regained some strength, I examined my feet. I had large blisters under my toes and on my heels. My swollen legs and my bruised feet were burning in pain. Under a tree, away from the road, I found myself a soft patch of green grass and fell asleep. I only heard a few cars pass on either side of the highway. When I woke, I felt a sharp pain in my back that slowly faded.

A terrible fear shocked my body, and horrible thoughts entered my mind. "No, please, God in Heaven, please don't let me have the baby here in the woods and alone." I cried in despair.

How I wished I could have stayed with my mother. I needed her so badly. I was all alone. When would I be able to smile freely again, if ever? When would I be able to eat food from a table, instead of garbage cans? Would I ever be able to sleep in a real bed, covered with soft sheets, blankets and feel safe again? There was no future to imagine. My instincts, fears, immaturity, survival, it all aimed towards saving the child I carried.

I often look back at myself, painfully getting off the ground, where I had spent that night. I thought I would die. I thought the time had come for me to leave this miserable world and step into another. It was only pain. I was still alive and ready to fight for another day. I tried to figure out the day when the baby was to come; How many more days left in this pregnancy, but I only knew it took about nine months to carry a child to full term. It was all a mystery to me.

I also did not know how far I was from the next city, or the name of the town. I stopped my walk and asked a farmer in the field. "The next town is Braunschweig, girl, and it is about a few hours away from here. You are not thinking of walking to Braunschweig, are you?" The farmer sounded friendly, and it also felt good to hear a friendly voice again. I also thought he was concerned about my well being. "Yes, I believe so," I answered, not knowing how long it would take me to get there. "Well, good luck to you, girl. You sure will need it," he replied as he shook his grey hair and turned back towards his chores.

There was little hope I would reach Braunschweig. My eyes were fixed on the road ahead of me. About every hour or so, I saw a car going in my direction, but somehow, I couldn't find the courage to thumb my way to the big city. I had no money to pay my fare. I did not know where to get things. Most of the stores in East Berlin were empty, and a person would obtain food with a ration card. Now on the open fields of the West, and small towns, I had not seen a store supplying food of any kind.

Not long after, a big truck passed me on the road and stopped. There it was parked on the side of the highway. It took me a while before I came close to it, and I did not feel like walking any further. I wondered if, perhaps, I could find the right words to ask the driver for a ride.

My reasoning was unsound. I changed my mind so many times.

For the first time in a long time, I noticed how poorly dressed I was. I didn't even have heels left on my shoes. I wondered what my face looked like. I had not seen myself in God knows how long. My clothes for that matter must have been quite a sight. I could only imagine the worst, but there was nothing I could do to improve my appearance. I was a refugee, poor, miserable and lonely.

I was almost beside the truck. I walked slowly, trying with all my might to find the right words to say. Was it perhaps possible that the driver was a woman? I could see someone on the side of the highway. This person seemed to be sitting there calmly, enjoying lunch. I guessed him to be no more than forty. As I got closer, I could see him pouring some kind of liquid into his cup. The man looked up at me and said, "You must have walked a long way and fast, too, to pass me." He spoke in a friendly voice, yet, I felt I could not trust him; though, I wanted to very much.

Somehow, my feet didn't want to carry me any further. My body and soul were exhausted. I sat down on the other side of him to watch his face and any move he could make. I watched him eating his sandwich and drink his coffee. My mouth was watering, yet I refused to ask for lunch. He then offered me one; I gratefully accepted it from his hands and gulped it quickly in case he changed his mind.

"How far are you going?" he asked.

"I have no destination," I replied.

"Where do you come from?" he quizzed.

"I crossed over the eastern border with a group of people, and we parted ways shortly after," I responded.

"Well, I am going to Braunschweig. If you want a lift, I can take you there," he offered.

"Is it the next biggest city?" I asked.

"Yes, it is, and it is safe for you. Perhaps, you should be in the city, that way if anything happens to you, you know?" he pointed.

I knew what he meant as I carried that worry with me all the time. I questioned myself as to whether or not I should take his offer or keep on walking. My conscience told me not to accept the offer and not to trust this man. Yet, I had to consider the long walk to the city. Also, I did not want to deliver my baby alone on the side of the road. Confused and reluctant, I accepted the offer of the ride to Braunschweig. I wanted to trust him. Perhaps, his being older made him wiser and more sympathetic towards my condition. He did have a point that taking him up on his offer was better than wandering alone in the countryside. Also, Braunschweig was a big city and only a stone throw away.

It had been a long time since I had been in a rolling truck, and it really felt good. I watched the scenery as we travelled past the fields. Though it was farmland, to me, it was beautiful. Seeing the trees along the route and not the rubble war had left behind was like a miracle. The farmhouses were not damaged. There were cows, horses and pigs left to graze on this fertile land. It seemed as if the war had not reached this far. Back in the East, the farmers had to leave their homestead. The area was left uncultivated, with no animals in sight. I wondered how long it would be before farmers ploughed the land again—years I assumed.

From far away, I heard the truck driver's voice. It brought me back to the present. He was speaking of his family and his friends still in East Germany. He spoke of their lives, which were in misery under the Russian rulers. I knew only too well the hardships they were living. Suddenly, I felt ashamed of myself for mistrusting him earlier. He seemed to understand the peoples' suffering in East and West Germany.

Suddenly, he slowed down the truck and came to a complete stop. "Just a bit of a stop," he explained. "I find it difficult on my eyes to stare in front while driving for so long."

I felt panic. My heart started to pound with that mistrusted feeling again. There were forty more miles before we arrived in Braunschweig. He wanted to rest, but his hands didn't quit. Perhaps, he now wanted to have sex in return for his eaten sandwich.

He asked, "what is the matter with you? All I ask for is a little kiss from you. You must understand that it has been a long time since I was home and with a woman. Besides, no one will know about it, nor is there any more harm to be done."

Any more harm, he referred to my already being pregnant. He wore this smirk smile on his face that made me feel inferior and worthless. I sat there motionless for a moment, stunned by his claim. When I regained my senses, I opened the truck door and jumped out in a hurry. Then I felt a horrible pain in my abdomen again, fell to the ground while he slammed the door shut and drove off.

While the pain was getting worse, I had to thank my blessings for not having to struggle with him further. Scrambling to the side of the road, I lay there, twisting and turning on the ground overtaken by this horrendous pain. It would leave for a short time only to return. I managed to get up and walk in a bent position holding my stomach with my arms straddled around and under my abdomen. Cars were passing by and ignoring me.

I noticed a Volkswagen parked a short distance ahead. I had not heard it nor seen it go by. A woman stepped out of the car and was walking towards me. When she reached me, she took my arms and helped me walk towards the Volkswagen. I could only feel gratitude towards this unfamiliar woman for her compassion. I silently thanked God for sending her my way.

"Where are you going?" she asked in a concerned tone. I explained to her that I wanted to reach Braunschweig.

Alarmed, she asked, "On foot! How far have you come from?"

"Yes, from the border!" I responded, trembling. At this point, I realized I had either a fever or my body was in shock because I could not stop myself from shaking.

"Are you cold, the lady asked as she sat next to me in the car?

"No, just a bit hot, I think," I said, shivering.

She then took a blanket from the back seat and wrapped me in it. While parked on the side of the highway, she promised she would take me to Braunschweig, even if she didn't have to go there. During our travel, she inquired about where I came from and other general questions about me. I blurted my story without fear or shame. An hour or more went by before we reached Braunschweig. It was dark by that time, and I did not know my way around Braunschweig too well.

The lady let me out of the car at the Railway Station. She stated she had to be on her way. I had nothing to offer her in terms of payment, but I did thank her warmly for her concern. I told her that perhaps one day we would meet again and I could return the favour to her. She smiled and said, "I don't think so, my dear, but God be with you. Goodbye!" I wondered if I would ever see her again, grateful for how my plans transformed so quickly. With all the people I met on my route, it was surprising to me how only a few offered to help.

I made my way to the waiting room inside the station, where it was warm, and I felt safe. It was crowded, smoky and smelled awful, but it felt familiar. I felt safe from men. Too many untrustworthy souls had crossed my path. I was not very efficient in recognizing when I was being entrapped or offered an act of kindness and preferred to be by myself.

Coming from East Berlin to the West seemed like I had crossed the ocean. The smell in the waiting room did not bother me anymore. I was tired, weary and didn't feel like speaking with anyone. I preferred to sit by myself. I found an empty table, sat down and lay my head on my arms to rest. I couldn't sleep right away, but I let my mind wander to the past few days since I had left East Germany. As I fell asleep, I hoped only to awake when all was okay again.

I was wakened by a lady officer asking me if I had a ticket. She had a stern sounding voice, and she had one of her hands on my shoulder. I noticed the police had made a ring around the railway station to capture the black market peddlers, prostitutes and others travelling without passports or identity papers. Again, the woman officer asked if I had a train ticket, a passport or some type of identification. Half asleep and stunned, I looked straight into her eyes and asked, "What for?"

"We will see what for," she said as she swung my chair around.

I realized now that she meant business. I quickly answered politely that I was sorry and that I had neither. Her voice was like one of a sergeant's when she ordered me to follow her. I did not dare ask her where to or what I had done. I knew this sweep was an attempt to gather the black market peddlers together.

I had experienced this kind of raid many times while in East Berlin. There were many prostitutes, and most girls did not have any type of health certification for proof that a doctor had checked them. I don't know which I found hardest, being pregnant, being ill, or lacking good food. I thought, if I was jailed, they were likely doing me a favour. All women ranged from ages fourteen to their fifties without proper identification, tickets or passports. Instead of the prison cell that I had expected, we were taken to a hospital to be examined by doctors for venereal diseases. The women were released if there wasn't evidence of ties with the black market or prostitution.

I was one of the last ones to enter the office. I had a check-up and answered some questions about my pregnancy. The doctor asked how far along I was with my pregnancy. With that many weeks without water and soap to keep myself clean and the shortage in underwear, I was sore between my thighs, infectious. The doctor wanted to be sure that it was nothing more than sores caused by the many miles of walking and a lack of hygiene. It took a while to complete all the tests.

When I returned to the waiting room, I expected to find the room empty. To my surprise, two women were waiting for me. They kept a group of women for the treatment of venereal diseases. I remember following the ladies to a room with twelve other women. I was done answering questions. No judgement.

What was more unusual was being given a towel, soap, a hospital gown, and a housecoat and then led to a small room with a tub. Ah, I felt safe, in a cocoon, free from the outside world. What pleasure and what a feeling I had as I stepped in the warm water. I soaped and rinsed myself several times, just enjoying the feel of the water. It had been a long time since I had the opportunity to clean my body with a whole soap to myself. The warmth of the water, the cleanliness of my surroundings; I felt like a new person as I made my way to my bed that night.

It was the middle of the night when a doctor shook me awake. I woke up all wet with sweat, trembling of fear and cold. The nightmares were just beginning. "Sorry to wake you," the doctor said, "but you were screaming." He left an order with the nurse to give me a sedative, but no sleep came. My dream, I recall, was of the Russians liberating Germany from the Nazi's. It filled my mind with the Red Army, the Cossacks; The rapes, the beatings, the clearing of the sick and dying in the hospital, the fleeing refugees, the dead left on the side of the road, in ditches, and that poor woman frozen in the snow while breastfeeding her child.

The next morning, I was the last one still sleeping as breakfast was served. None of the girls paid attention to me nor did any ask questions. The doctor did return before the end of his working hours to see if I would talk about it. He was very caring. He left by saying things would get better in time. "You will forget as years go by."

My five days in the hospital were comforting. When it came time to leave, they offered precious gifts. They gave me underwear, a fresh bar of soap and a comb. They had also cleaned my clothes.

Once declared fit enough, I was brought to a home for unwed mothers in Hildesheim. After a short stay, I woke up one morning, not knowing where I was, with horrible pain. I walked for a while along a corridor. There were different attendants here, mostly women: nurses, wet nurses, midwives and the odd doctor. As a nurse walked towards me, I explained the terrible pain in my abdomen and lower back. She led me to the delivery room.

The pain was so intense that walking around the room was much better than lying in bed. After having labour pains every two minutes, I would stretch out over a railing at the foot of the bed. The nurse then insisted I stay in bed and let her guide me through it.

I cried for my mother. I felt I was losing myself. Something else had taken over my body. The bitter me would not lie helpless, in that bed, crying for my mother. The woman had abandoned me, a fourteen-year-old child alone on the streets of horror, in a war-torn country. Now, I was to become a mother at eighteen without her guidance, love or support.

Soon after, my water broke. Ah, the shame! I thought I had wet the bed and did not want the doctor to take the cover off of me. Among strangers, my baby was born. On March 1st, 1951, I gave birth to Wilfred Möwis, a 6 lbs baby boy. "Yes, it's a boy," the doctor answered my silent question. All I could make out was a dark film around the baby's body. Relieved and exhausted from labour, came an angry cry.

For a while, I was no longer angry with the world. Now, there was someone to take care of besides me. There was someone to love, someone that needed my love, a reason to live. I felt so happy for a short time. It was only a small dream. I recovered from an illness caused by starvation, hunger for love and a continuous struggle for survival.

A few weeks following this episode of my life, I left my baby at the home for unwed mothers. I had to establish myself in a life where I could care for my child. Most unwed mothers who left home, were not only looking for food and money to survive but also for a man to cling to. Most of us looked for anything away from the streets. Most German men hoped for a better life in another country or just everyday work. It was not love we looked for; it was raw survival.

The only safe place I could think of, at that moment in time, was the refugee camps. On the western side, you had to pay to stay in one overnight. The A.M.P. (American Military Police) had a hard time keeping the German girls out of their soldier's camp. We did try our luck. The women of the streets all felt the same pain: hunger, safety, basic human needs. But, I moved on.

# CHAPTER THIRTEEN

# Living in the West

*M*y travels took me to a camp called "The Falling Hostel" in Luneburg. Right next to the Railway line, was a refugee camp. To stay overnight, you had to pay fifty cents. It included a meal served in the evening that was much more substantial than the piece of rye bread and watery soup of East Germany. I would beg all day, from door to door, for food or money so I would have a roof over my head at night. After learning the ropes to survive in the West, I noticed that the garbage bins of the Americans were much better than the Russian's garbage in the East. However, they were stricter as to keeping the street people away. There were more soldiers to chase us.

Soon, I became acquainted with a German soldier that had been in the war. He had lost a leg and had been a prisoner of war with the Russians. Before the war, he had been a Game-Keeper in Ostpreussen. How little he had now. He taught me how to become a beggar. We posed as man and wife. We walked miles every day, begging door to door and on the streets for pennies, nickels and dimes. We worked hard to pick up enough money for the refugee camp and the evening meal at night. But he was getting serious about our arrangement and wanted to marry me. It made me sick to my stomach, posing as man and wife. I did not want to stay with him. I did not want to be begging for food for the rest of my life. After a few weeks, I told him I was sick and would not follow him that day. Without warning or goodbyes, I set out on my own towards the farming community. I had decided I would try the begging routine on my own.

"I am a refugee, and I am starving. I beg you, please, for a sandwich or ten cents to help pay for my stay in the refugee camp."

One of the first farmers I encountered that day replied: "If your hungry girl, would you be willing to work for it. I will feed you three meals a day and give you a bed."

"Happily," I answered.

I could not believe my good fortune. The farmer invited me into his home, where he introduced his wife and three children. Later, I met the farm hand I would be replacing, Gertrude. After dinner and chores were over, we took the time to get acquainted. They asked the same questions I was asked about everywhere. "Where are you from? Where are your parents? Where is your family?"

After listening to my story, the farmer said, satisfied. "You had your share of hardship, more than anyone here ever lived. I asked the same question to all the begging refugees that come to my door for food," he told me.

At night, Gertrude and I got together and became good friends. She showed me to my room and told me why she was leaving. She also showed me my work, which she was doing at the time. From that day on, I never returned to a refugee camp. I was free to go where I wanted, and I had nothing left behind to collect. It felt like a new beginning, and I thought it was the start of my destiny. Now there was a purpose, someone to live for.

The room in which I slept was behind bags of oats and barley and stacks of hay for the horses. For the first two days, the work was reasonable because Gertrude and I shared the work between us. The farmer himself would help us with the heavy stuff. He helped teach me to feed the horses, milk the six cows, feed potatoes to the pigs and feed the chickens with table scraps and grains. Little did I realize that when Gertrude left, I would have to do the work on my own.

The last night that Gertrude slept there, I asked her where she was going and why. "I would stay, but they fired me. I need more than just the use of a bed to sleep in at night. You don't get paid for your work. You only get a bed and something to eat three times a day, which isn't enough for the work they expect you to do. So, I stole grain and feed and sold it. I saved enough to go where I want to go. I have a friend in Bergen-Belsen. She works there for a Jewish family, and she wrote that she found work for me with a family. That's where I'm going. At least I will be able to earn money."

I did not interrupt her while she spoke, but I was thinking of my child, which was still at the home for unwed mothers. Later, I realized the meaning of what she was saying, and I felt like leaving myself.

The next morning, Gertrude was gone, and the work waited to be done. At six o'clock, the farmer called me out of bed. I got dressed and went out to the barn to milk the cows with him. I had never done farm work before, and after the first week, my body ached all over. I was still too slow to catch up to the farmer. I milked one cow while he did three. The wet tail of the cows would blind me as it whipped me in the face, and too often, the cows would kick the bucket and spill the milk. He would then leave me alone to finish and go in for breakfast and then went to work at another farm. When I finally finished milking the remaining cows, I hurried in for breakfast and then returned to my chores. I fed the chickens and the rabbits. I filled a boiler with potatoes to cook for the next day and then fed the pigs with what was called a mash. Afterwards, I had to clean the stalls of the animals with a shovel.

Come lunchtime, the farmer's wife would appear with a packed lunch. She would watch me while I ate. She would then repack the containers, and she would return to the house. The afternoon usually ended with the children coming to watch me exercise the horses and brush them down. After supper, we repeated the work with the cows. It was a never-ending job. There was no one with whom to socialize. The farmer and his wife seemed satisfied with my work. After my arrival, weeks went by, and I never heard a kind word of encouragement from my employers. The only real human contacts were the children.

Johan was five years old and very talkative, always questioning, and full of life. He had the charge of his younger brother, David, who was barely out of diapers. The eldest boy rambled on about the antics of his brother and how he had a hard time playing the games he wanted to play while following his little brother. Too funny, how serious he was about his responsibility. He was a leader, and the younger one followed wherever he went. His topic of choice was to get his younger brother to grow up to his level. David had to be watched so he would not get hurt or break his favourite toys. The children were a fresh break from the hard work of a farmhand, and I enjoyed their banter. I had my own child still waiting for me to come and get him, and I would need to be able to care for him.

I had been hoping for a letter from Gertrude. She had promised to keep in touch after she had settled in her new home and work, to let me know if there were any openings for work. I would go out to the street at times to meet the mailman at the road but always left disappointed. Later, I found out a letter had come in the first week after Gertrude's departure, but I had never received it. Finally, a second letter did arrive almost a month after she had left. It was the first letter for me since leaving my home town of Landsberg.

Gertrude was apologizing for not writing sooner but had been kept quite busy.

*Dear Anne,*

*There are a few openings here to work with Jewish families waiting for immigration papers to the Holy land or different parts of America. There is hatred for the Germans, but I did not realize what the concentration camps were. The food is good, and there is room to live with the families until they leave. It is a small city. There are American and English soldiers and a Casern nearby. The city also has a movie theatre and a dance hall. Most evenings, we are free. Please try to let me know if you have received my first letter or if you are coming.*

*Gertrude*
*Bergen-Belsen*

Having had such good news, I was in a rush to leave. That last day at the farm was a very long one. I rushed through my chores in a daze. My mind was just preoccupied with plans. After supper, I wrapped my belongings and thought of confronting the farmer and his wife about the first letter that came. I decided not to bother.

When I first accepted the job, leaving the refugee camp, I was hungry and desperate to leave my life as a refugee. As a farmhand, I thought I would enjoy being with animals on a farm. It would have been a nice place to raise a child on my own. As it turned out, the work atmosphere was just not for me. I left the farm in the middle of the night without giving notice and thumbed away on the Autobahn. No one knew I was coming, but I found my way to Bergen-Belsen.

During the Nazi power, Bergen-Belsen had a concentration camp with a military station that kept watch over it, three miles away. No longer a German military station, I found Jewish families awaiting their papers to immigrate to the western world. The barrack was quite large, with many rooms that had housed two to four German soldiers per room. I had dared to enter the lion's den to find a place to work. German Jewish families employed German girls to help with their household chores. I was hired to work for a Jewish family that was waiting on their immigration papers.

My friend Gertrude was disappointed that I had not contacted her before coming. I had spent my first evening with her, and she came with me to meet my new employer.

Mrs. Grauss was a young woman of about 32 years old. She had two daughters of school age and a little boy of two. Her husband was away on business and only returned on Friday afternoons. They were both very friendly and never spoke of their days in the concentration camp. My only chores were the housework and the care of the children. There were three rooms; one was used for the kitchen, while the other two were bedrooms. Mr. and Mrs. Grauss slept in one bedroom, and the children slept in the other while I slept in the kitchen. The kitchen was big enough to have a bed in the corner by the window.

On Saturdays, when done with the dishes, I would go out for a walk with the children around the neighbourhood. At first, I thought nothing of it, but I often met a guard by the name of Nicholi (Klaus) Spurdza. I greeted him politely, as he had helped me when I was searching for my friend Gertrude the first day I arrived. Nicholi opened a conversation and invited me to the dance hall for that evening. I couldn't look into his dark brown eyes; I had a feeling of anxiety and nervousness. I stuttered with my words, tormented by all the mishaps I had had in the past. I walked away in embarrassment without giving him an answer.

Mrs. Grauss noticed that I was acting strange that evening. "Are you not feeling well, Anneliese," she asked with concern. I was lost in thoughts when I answered her, "Oh no, I am feeling fine," as I avoided her eyes. I was planning for a way to get my son back and thought perhaps I would need help from a man.

One day upon entering the market, I found farmers conducting sales of vast amounts of vegetables and fruits. Nicholi (Klaus) Spurdza was in uniform with American markings. He had an accent, but something told me he was not American. He was from the Ukraine. He was just slightly taller than me, well built, healthy, with dark brown hair and brown eyes. He invited me out on a date to see a movie. It was the beginning of a love-hate relationship that we both entered with heavy baggage.

Nicholi was born in the Ukraine, in 1924. He mentioned that he had been abandoned by his parents as a baby and left on a doorstep. The story was a bit ambiguous. At the age of 14, he had joined the military. Later, he worked for an underground partisan against the Nazis. He was trained to kill. The couple that raised him was referred to as aunt and uncle and later as Opa and Oma. Oma and Opa had made their way to Germany, from the Ukraine, to visit with Nicholi before immigrating to Canada. They offered to sponsor Nicholi to come and join them.

My present situation with the Jewish Grauss family, and being away from a child that I wanted with me, led me to blindly having a relationship with Klaus. He was very demanding sexually, and I did my best to oblige, but my heart and past experience with men kept me hesitant. In the meantime, the Grauss family received their notice to immigrate to the United States. I applied for a room to live nearby until I could find new employment. They accepted my application. Nicholi visited often and frequently spent the night. We argued and fought often, and his angry streak would end up in a beating.

It did not take long to realize I was pregnant again. The beatings continued. Later, we were married by paper only. This marriage was only half of our marital status: no ceremony, no food, no guests, no celebration. We moved to a small apartment in a building for married American soldiers. Frightened and sick to my stomach, I did not feel like a bride. It was November when Nicholi decided to take his aunt's and uncle's offer to sponsor him to Canada. He applied for a passport for me and prepared the paperwork for sponsoring me to immigrate as well. Together, we returned to Hildesheim for my seven-month-old son Wilfred.

Till now, I had made myself believe I could trust a man again. I was so wrong. One of his habits in the morning was getting dressed in his uniform. But, before he left for work, he would grab me, pull my clothes off, throw me on the chesterfield and have his way with me. If I resisted in any way, he would slap my face, throw me on the floor and kick me, he would respond with, "You have a kid, take care of him," without any mind to the child I was carrying. He had a bad habit of kicking my buttocks as I passed by him. He had very little respect for me.

I still hated all men and their desire for love and mating. I felt that, perhaps, if Nicholi understood my feelings, he would not have been so angry at my lack of affection. After putting the little one to bed one evening, my husband sat next to me on the chesterfield. He shared his belief that I was no different than any other woman and that I did not love him but was looking for a meal ticket. Deep down in my heart, I knew he was right. I did not love him, and I was looking for a way to a better life.

I felt so confused and misunderstood. He would laugh at me and ask where else could I go. He warned me to behave and threatened death if I stepped out of line, reminding me of his training to kill and his power to have me and my son disappear. "I was better with him than out on the streets," he would remind me. Nicholi worked for the Americans as a mechanic, a chauffeur, and periodically as a guard. He never disclosed any other purpose to his work.

Peter was born on May 4, 1951, in Bergen-Belsen, Germany. A midwife delivered the baby. No complications. Nothing out of the ordinary took place. I had accepted my fate, and I was ready for what life had to offer.

Several months later, Nicholi received his papers of acceptance to immigrate to Canada. In November, within three days, he was off to his new country. I had to stay in Germany, but I could not remain in the soldiers' compound for soldier's families. I was accepted to wait for my final papers in the barrack, then called an immigration camp. I was given a room for my two baby boys and I. There were several women in the same predicament as I was. I was content enough. Looking after the boys, I made a few girlfriends.

Meals were served in a common room. The worse was lining up to collect our meals while the boys waited in the room for my return. The nights were hard. We had a bad infestation of bed bugs. The boys were the worst when they were full of bug bites. Every morning at two am, they would turn on the lights in the rooms. The idea here was to grab your slipper and start killing the bugs crawling along the walls. A hilarious sight, I would say, as you could hear the slapping of many slippers along the corridor. That was my life that winter and spring until a letter came one day, explaining my imminent departure to the new world.

Fear and worry of the unknown filled my mind as I prepared to leave. And so, in early July of 1952, I packed a small suitcase and found my way to new adventures in Canada.

CHAPTER FOURTEEN

# Canada

*As she was presented with the framed picture of the ship that she had called The General Von Taylor, Anne read the caption on the bottom of the image. "Crossing the Atlantic: Anne Möwis Pitt crossed with her two boys Wilfred and Peter in 1952." Tears flowed down her face.*

*****

*J*never looked at the ship. I had one baby in one arm, a suitcase in the other, and Wilfred holding on to my coat when we left the Immigration camp. Wilfred was fussing every step of the way to the train wanting to be in my arms too. Our new adventure had not started very well. We made our way to the Bremerhaven Station, a port city situated on the North Sea coast, without further incidence. The ship was there," she said, "and I was just concentrating on getting on board.

On the ship, we were given a cabin that contained a set of bunk beds with a sink and toilet. As in the immigration camp, the routine was quite the same, but I was surrounded by strangers. I was on my own and feared the unknown. I was apprehensive about the reception that awaited us in Canada. I had had no correspondence with Nicholi since he had left me back in Germany.

Our meals were taken in the cabin. I had to leave the children every morning to go pick up their food in the kitchen area for eight am. There usually was a short line up, but everything was a rush to get back to the children. After getting Wilfred and Peter dressed and settled for a nap, I would rush out again to collect my breakfast. I was washing diapers every day, bathing them in the sink, rushing out for meals and taking them on short walks. Often, as I rushed out to get my own breakfast, I would be too late and had to do without my morning meal.

After their bedtime, I would make sure they were sleeping and sneak out to watch the entertainment for a bit. People gathered in a small room on our level of the ship where men with a squeezebox would play music and couples danced. A young man named Kurt approached me, and we got to dancing and talking about our lives and future.

The next ten days were uneventful, though. I had met someone to say hello to and chat. Little did I know that he would later find his way to London to check up on me. When we left the ship, I never turned back to look around. Getting to where I was going and focusing on the boys, took all my attention.

Arriving in Halifax, we were led to a big room with tables, and we were lined up for interviews. Then, one by one, we were told where to proceed, as people were questioned and sent on their way. There were translators; I could not understand a word they were saying. It did not take long to proceed to the train.

Inside the train, we were led to another cabin with two benches, given a pillow for the three of us: no blankets, no food, no water. It was frustrating. I had such a hard time because of the language barrier. Before bed, I made myself understood; the children were hungry. The train attendant found us a sandwich for the three of us. We travelled to London, Ontario, that night. Tending to the boys was my priority. They needed to be settled in somewhere, and I needed to feel safe. The train finally arrived in London the next day.

Being in Canada, seeing so many trees and strange houses, everything was new, unfamiliar and piquing my interest. We had arrived. We were home. Little did I know what was waiting for the three of us.

When we came off the train, I did not feel good. I was hungry and lost. A policeman noticed our disorientation and questioned us. Not understanding English, I pointed to my little card, which was pinned on my dress. On this card, he obtained the information about where we were going. He figured where we wanted to go and called a taxi. This was my first time in a taxi, and I was more or less afraid for the children and myself being in the hands of a stranger. After we went in one block and out the other, I relaxed enough that I could look away from the window. There was no reason to be afraid. Finally, we stopped, arriving at our destination.

I was still filled with worry as my husband was not aware of our arrival. I did not know how he would accept this. He must have had a reason for not writing. Perhaps, he did not intend to bring us to Canada. I had to satisfy the uncertainty in my heart. The driver helped us into the house where Nicholi, who in Canada had changed his name to Klaus, lived with his uncle, whom we referred to as Opa and his aunt as Oma.

Thank God for this, as they made us feel welcomed with acts of kindness. I was overwhelmed with exhaustion when I broke down and cried but pleased to have reached my destination safely and in good health.

Klaus was at work, and I was not entirely comfortable as it created stress for me. While the children were fed and washed then put to bed, I learned from Oma that he had been working for the past six months. He had been working in a lumber camp. They had not taken any rent money from him, for they would rather see him bring us from overseas as soon as possible. "I had no idea that you were coming that soon," she said, surprised. "Klaus must have placed all his money in the bank and kept it a secret that you were coming, the devil," she went on laughing.

Klaus arrived later that afternoon. He did not expect my arrival. No arrangements had been made for living quarters. He did, however, have a room somewhere.

There was no welcoming committee, and things were awkward. The baby, Peter, was crawling on the floor the afternoon of our arrival. He tried to stand holding on to a glass coffee table, it tilted. Klaus grabbed him and started giving him a beating. He was barely a year old. Crying myself and hearing the screams of my child who did not even know his father was devastating. Not understanding what was happening to him, my child was trying to reach for me as he was being yelled at and slapped over and over again. That's what I remember from my first day in Canada.

We were made to feel we were my husband's property, and he could do to us what he felt was best. We stayed at the in-laws that night because the room where Klaus lived was not suitable for the children. The next day, we left to find a place to live, buy food and essentials.

It was a difficult adjustment because we had nothing but a bed, a chest of drawers, a suitcase and our clothes. With the help of Oma and Opa and their friends, we managed. We settled in a small, two-bedroom upstairs apartment in London. Klaus left for work the next week, and I did my best to settle in. Not long after, he got a new job with Calvinator Refrigeration.

I had come a long way to find out the shocking story about my husband. He had left Germany seven months before me. One afternoon, shortly after he had gone to work, I was surprised by a visitor at my door. It was a woman who introduced herself as a friend of my husband. I invited her in for tea. The lady was a bit younger than me and looked very friendly. She had sad eyes, and she said she had wanted to meet me, but I could tell she was upset and she spoke German, so I was happy to oblige. Her visit was not a happy one. Her news was that she was pregnant with my husband's child and that they had been seeing each other for a few months. I wish I could have told her that she could have him. What a mess!

I kept my eyes on the baby's face in my arms when I announced to him what I knew. I knew his angry eyes were studying me. I did not dare look into his face. I kept my eyes fixed on Peter. It made Klaus angrier by the second. The pressure was building, and he could not stand that he was under attack. I could not get myself to look at him when he was talking so close to me. I could not stand his hateful remarks. Frightening seconds passed as he expected me to say something. Trembling, I waited for his fleshy callous hand to smash into the side of my face. When it came, as I use to do when my mother backhanded me, I walked away and closed myself in the children's room. I heard the door slam, and he was gone.

I tried to avoid confrontations where I could. Nothing seemed to matter to me but the children. I had never felt wanted or loved, but I had a deep warm feeling for the boys. They were well behaved, quiet boys. They also had fear in their heart. They feared their father. Things were quiet when we were alone, which was most of the time.

Being in a new place on my own, I did not adventure far. The language barrier was atrocious. My husband spoke Ukrainian with his family, and they only spoke German when they were addressing me. Before speaking to Klaus about my going to work, I had asked Oma if she would watch the children while I went out to pick apples in the fall. She was more than happy to do so. Then I had to approach Klaus, and he warmed to the idea. The farmer would pick me up at the door, and I would come home with a bag full of apples. Klaus got paid for my work because I never received any money.

One year passed in our married life in Canada together, and I did not remember a day with him without arguments, fights or beatings. Klaus, my husband would get jealous of anything. I had to weigh my words and put everything I said on a scale, making sure I would not say too much or say things that would upset him. "I will kill you and the children if you even think of leaving me," he grabbed his coat and slammed out the door as he left. I don't know what we had argued about. I was too tired to try to think about why.

Wilfred, Peter and I were on pins and needles in his company. We would close ourselves in the boys' bedroom. I would kneel on the floor and pray. "Please, God, help me make it go, not for me, but for the two little souls of my boys".

In Germany, as a refugee, I had been cold and hungry, I feared for my tomorrows. Now I asked for the strength to stop making him angry. I can hardly remember the times when the sun was shining for me.

One night, he had been working late and I could hear knocking on the door at the bottom of the stairs of our building. I had been in bed, so I hurried up to get my housecoat on and rush down the stairs. He was so angry that I had not been there faster to open the door. I did not make it far. Someone else had let him in. The door to our apartments was locked after ten in the evening. Klaus was furious when he got into the apartment, embarrassed at having disturbed the neighbours. I had been too slow to answer the door. I tried to make him understand that I had not been responsible for the turn of events, and he just turned on me.

That night the neighbours called the police for a disturbance. Defending myself was no option; he had lost all sense of control. He threw me on the floor and just kicked and punched while I yelled and cried until someone came to stop him. He had more to be ashamed of, but he could not seem to accept any responsibility for his actions.

While the police stood by and watched Klaus, I cleaned myself up as well as I could. My next step was to pack a bag for the children and one for myself. Preparing the children and trying to reassure them, took all the courage I could muster.

Exhausted as I was, the police officers helped me to their car and drove us to a church that was known to help victims of abuse.

On a church bench, I settled the boys with a pillow for the night. Not long after, I set my head on my rolled-up coat and passed out. Almost one year after landing in Canada, I found myself destitute and back out on the streets, this time with my two boys and a language barrier. Peter was two and a half, Wilfred was four.

I received help, but making myself understood was very difficult. Half the time, I did not know who I was talking to or who I was dealing with. I ended up living in a one-bedroom living quarter, across from a restaurant. Our new home had a hotplate, a small table and chair, a chesterfield and a bed; Oh, and a television.

I do not know how that came about, but for the next week, I felt rich and safe. The boys would sleep on the chesterfield, and I had the bed. They soon learned to share the bed with me. When I wanted to stay up later to watch television, they would go to sleep in my bed, and I would sleep on the chesterfield. Soon, I realized that I would need to work to feed them and remain in the apartment.

An older couple lived in an apartment on the same level that I lived on. They were very helpful and friendly. They agreed to watch the children while I applied for a job across the street at the restaurant. Having no television of their own, which was quite a novelty at the time, they were very happy to be able to come and watch their favourite programs. And thus, I was able to make arrangements for employment.

However, I still had a big challenge with the language barrier; I set myself up to practice my English while watching television. Refining my waitressing skills became another challenge I had to overcome. To take orders, I would ask the customers to write down their orders for food, giving them a seating arrangement. It worked for me. Mistakes were few and far between. My take-home pay at the time was a few dollars a week living on the tips. The manager was satisfied with my work ethics, but it was never enough to make ends meet.

There was another challenge I had a hard time shaking; Klaus was stalking me. As I was working in the restaurant one late afternoon, Klaus came in and insisted on speaking to the manager. According to my boss, he warned them that I should be fired as I was going to ruin their reputation. He told them that I was a prostitute and good for nothing. The manager told him that they were satisfied with my work, and what I did away from the restaurant was none of their business. If there was an issue, they would deal with it at the time. Things did not end there. He wanted to punish me for leaving him.

The time came for my eldest son, Wilfred, to start school. He was five at the time, and I registered him for his first day. At the same time, I was accepted to work in exchange for a reduced fee for my son's tuition. It was still too hard to make ends meet. I still had a hard time with the language barrier and did not know my rights or of any available welfare service. My options were limited in my mind.

I spoke to the teacher about my difficulties in finding a good babysitter and meeting my financial responsibilities. The teacher convinced me that the best course of action was to give up my children to adoption. Thus, they would receive a better chance in life.

With her help, I tried to get Klaus to sign papers as he had the first right to his son Peter. He refused and took Peter back to raise himself. The last memory of my son Peter as I was collecting the remainder of my clothes and Wilfred's in Klaus' apartment was a tearful three-year-old crying, "Don't leave me, mommy, don't leave. Mommy come home." He was sitting on the back top of a living room chair.

My eldest son Wilfred was adopted through private adoption. The school teacher knew people that wanted to adopt. Still, spending the day with 5-year-old children and working at the restaurant in addition to that, was wearing me down. Filling the proper papers and promising not to see or contact my son in any way, was heartbreaking.

The exchange was done through a lawyer, and as I left the building, I ran a few miles back to my home, crying my heart out. I wrapped myself in my blankets in bed until sleep took over.

I thought of my past life and the only man that had always been compassionate with me, Vincent Jacobolski. Wilfred had been conceived in love. Life could have been different if he had survived. He did not even have time to know he was going to be a father. But life goes on, and I had to work with what I had. My search for love was a driving force. Depressed, lost, and no one to turn to, I decided to make my way to Toronto and find a job in a new town.

My life and the living nightmare from the past still haunt me today. There were more nightmares to come. It was not easy for me at first, as I had many challenges to face. However, not all is lost. I still have my memories, as vivid as if they had happened yesterday. Though, I can freely share my experiences without feeling fear of retaliation. I have learned to love and understand my new country.

Anne and her sister Dora, Landsberg-on-the-Warta, circa 1944

Anne and Gertrude working for Jewish families, 1950 in Bergen- Belsen

Anne and Nicholi (far right) with two boys (front center) in London Ontario with family and friends 1953-54

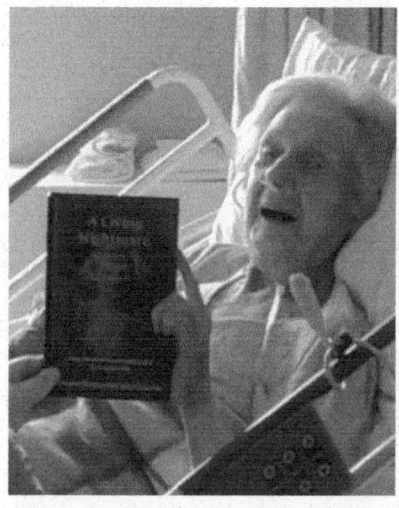

*Anneliese Möwis Pitt passed away at the Timmins District Hospital on June 12, 2020. Anne was born in Germany in 1929. She leaves behind her sons Peter Spurdza (Sherry Bradette), David Stewart (alias Wilfred Möwis) (Jamie York), her grandchildren Cheryl Mandeville, Joel and David Castonguay, Melinda Stewart, Tammy Knox and great-grandchildren Devon, Samantha, and Aolani.*

*Anneliese will be profoundly missed by her endearing friend Ghislaine Raymond. Her long-lasting wish was to have her early life story told in a book. She had the opportunity to blissfully hold her book, "A Living Nightmare", two days prior to her passing.*

*A genuine thank you to the staff at Timmins District Hospital for their care and compassion during Anne's long convalescence.*

# Acknowledgements

*We spent a lot of time going back and forth between Anneliese (Anne), Ghislaine (Jess) and Laurette (Laure). Sharing tears, trying to imagine or for Anne reliving what it was like as a child to leave the necessities of life, to living without adult direction, on the streets of a war-torn country. With this conscionable torment in mind, Jess and Laure would first and foremost like to thank Anneliese for her endless patience with our troubling inquiries to further enlighten us on the events she outlined.*

*We also wish to express our gratitude to Anne's sons, Peter and David, for their support to tell her story.*

*Thank you to our husbands, Leonard and Paul, for their unlimited patience. A very special thank you to the following persons for their input and words of encouragement: Leona Joannette, Jocelyne McConnell, Natalie Raymond and Lise Legault.*

*A very special thank you to Kim Carroccio for her hours of revising and structuring our final version.*

*A very precious thank you to each other, sisters Jess and Laure, for working endlessly in a pleasant and considerate presence.*

*God bless all who have suffered or selflessly helped in any way big or small during wartimes. May our children continue to live in peaceful times always...*